PEDRO ALMODÓVAR

INTERVIEWS

CONVERSATIONS WITH FILMMAKERS SERIES
PETER BRUNETTE, GENERAL EDITOR

Photo credit: Photofest

PEDRO
ALMODÓVAR
INTERVIEWS

EDITED BY
PAULA WILLOQUET-MARICONDI

UNIVERSITY PRESS OF MISSISSIPPI / JACKSON

www.upress.state.ms.us

Publication of this book was made possible in part by a grant from the Program for Cultural Cooperation between Spain's Ministry of Education, Culture and Sports, and United States Universities.

The University Press of Mississippi is a member of the Association of American University Presses.

11 10 09 08 07 06 05 04 03   4 3 2 1
∞
Library of Congress Cataloging-in-Publication Data

Almodóvar, Pedro.
    Pedro Almodóvar : interviews / edited by Paula Willoquet-Maricondi.
        p.   cm.—(Conversations with filmmakers series)
    Includes index.
    ISBN 1-57806-568-2 (cloth : alk. paper)—ISBN 1-57806-569-0 (pbk. : alk. paper)
    1. Almodóvar, Pedro—Interviews.   2. Motion picture producers and directors—Spain—Interviews.   I. Willoquet-Maricondi, Paula, 1960–
II. Title.   III. Series
PN1998.3.A46A5   2004
791.43'0233'092—dc21   2003049711

British Library Cataloging-in-Publication Data available

CONTENTS

INTRODUCTION

''FROM RAGS TO RICHES'' may be a melodramatic way to put it, but it is not all that inaccurate a description of Pedro Almodóvar's journey from a small urban town in La Mancha to Madrid, from a humble provincial upbringing to international acclaim as Spain's leading postmodern *auteur*. It is no surprise, then, that time and time again interviewers probe Almodóvar about his origins and personal life, and celebrate his relatively quick international success against many odds, including his lack of formal training in film, the financial constraints under which he has had to work, the very limitations imposed by the Spanish film industry, and even his artistic and personal eccentricities. "It is a surprise that I'm making movies," he admits in a 1996 interview with *Film Journal International*, "because in my case it was almost impossible to dream of that. I was not born in the right place in the right family in the right town in the right language or in the right moment to make movies."

When asked about his family, his religious upbringing, his early infatuation with cinema, and his involvement in Madrid's underground artistic movement, Almodóvar generously obliges his interviewers. He likes to discuss his sense of always having been somewhat of an outsider, an "extraterrestrial," as he once put it. "It's clear that I bother many people . . . I remember that in school I inspired the same rejection in most of my classmates that I now can inspire in the critics," he confesses in a 1984 interview with *El País*. Even today, in spite of his tremendous box office success, international recognition, and many awards, Almodóvar feels misunderstood. The source of this misunderstanding is, paradoxically, his very fame, which seems to have forced him into a kind of isolation, or so he claims. "I'm a lone wolf and I'm getting to be more secretive. It's not in my nature; it's the fault of this damn fame," he explains in a 1999 interview with the French film journal, *Positif*. However, the very existence of the present collection of interviews is a testament to the fact that Almodóvar is neither shy about being interviewed nor secretive about his personal and professional life.

As Almodóvar's biographical details that surface in each of the interviews suggest, some of the key ingredients for his success were already in place by the time he moved alone to Madrid at the age of sixteen. His early exposure to and passion for cinema (which he regards as his true education), his innate talent for singing and telling stories, his formal academic education (unusual for someone of his socio-economic background), and his courageous and adventurous spirit were all significant contributing factors to his creativity, productivity, and success. Even Almodóvar's share of personal dramatic experiences, including a sexual incident involving a priest at one of the Catholic schools he attended, have been productively channeled into his films, sometimes in surprising ways. He admits that all of his films are very personal, biographical even, and that there is a little of him in all his characters. His visceral cinema is a blend of melodrama, humor, and excess that are deployed in the service of a deeply felt sense of empathy for the marginalized and the misunderstood.

Whether or not Almodóvar would describe his personal trajectory as the stuff from which melodramas are made, melodrama is, without a doubt, one of the defining modalities of his cinema, already in evidence as early as his third feature length film, *Dark Habits*. Infused with what he calls an "obvious sentimentality," *Dark Habits* "certainly is a melodrama," he says; but, he adds, with a dose of humor that "is a less corrosive kind of humor, less wacky than in the case of *Pepi* . . . or *Labyrinth* . . . in which, additionally, feelings were not discussed."

While classical Hollywood melodrama has never ceased to hold a tremendous appeal for Almodóvar, one of the recurring motifs in the interviews collected here is his refusal to be bound by any one genre. Adhering to one genre at the exclusion of all others is too limiting for this expansive autodidact filmmaker, writer, and performer. What he proclaims to like about the "extreme genres" (e.g. melodrama) is the opportunity they afford him to "talk naturally about strong sentiments without a sense of the ridiculous." An additional factor he often discusses to explain his characteristically postmodern transgression of genres is his self-proclaimed "amorality." As he explains in a lengthy interview with *Film Quarterly* published in 1987, "You can say my films are melodramas, tragicomedies, comedies or whatever because I used to put everything together and even change genre within the same sequence and very quickly. But the main difference is the private morality. When I say morality, I don't mean ethics, it's just a private point of view." Almodóvar crosses and bends genres because he prefers to work within his own morality or rather, *outside* morality. "I like melodramas," Almodóvar exuberantly admits in a 1988 interview, "but I can't actually make a big melodrama because my point of view is amoral."

However acceptable (or tolerated) Almodóvar's "personal morality" or "amorality" may have become since his rise to fame in 1984 with the commercial success in Spain of *What Have I Done to Deserve This?*, his unrepentant liberalism was not easily embraceable in the late Franco years. When, in the early 1970s, Almodóvar started producing mostly short and provocative Super-8 films, writing for underground magazines under the pseudonym Patty Diphusa, and playing in a punk-rock band, freedom of artistic expression was still severely limited by censorship and the suspension of civil liberties. His black and white, mostly silent, low budget films focused on controversial subjects like homosexuality, transexuality, scatology, sadomasochism, drugs, rape, and incest. These themes continue to infuse his films, even today, and give them that certain "Almodóvarian" quality that is discussed in the interviews.

These early films were the expression of a politically charged defiance of authority by a rising "new Spanish mentality" bent on overcoming boundaries and taboos. With incendiary titles like *Two Whores or Love Story Ending in a Wedding* (1974), *The Fall of Sodom* (1975), *Sex Comes, Sex Goes* (1977), *Fuck, Fuck, Fuck Me Tim!* (1978), these early ventures into filmmaking not only foreshadowed, but marked and celebrated the abolition of censorship and the belated rise in Spain of the punk, hippie, feminist, and gay liberation movements after Franco's death in 1975. Symptomatic of the *Movida*—the 1970s vanguard underground artistic wave that blasted the sexual and cultural mores of Franco's Spain—Almodóvar's early films were the repository of his distinctive and provocative thematic repertoire. His first commercial foray in 1980, a 16 mm full-length feature entitled *Pepi, Luci, Bom . . .* , received wide public exposure and began earning him interviews in mainstream Spanish film journals.

The 1981 interview for *Contracampo* that opens this volume is among the first ones to appear in Spain and traces many of Almodóvar's central thematic and stylistic concerns: sexuality, scatology, marginality, pop culture and advertising, Madrid's underground, urban life, family, religion, melodrama, and the universe of the housewife. Almodóvar addresses these themes in the course of his twenty-two-year directorial career, which comprises fourteen commercial features to date. Among the most frequently discussed topics in the twenty interviews collected here are religion and the world of the housewife. Starting in the late 1980s, the focus of the interviews shifts toward discussions of the evolution of his style, his cinematic techniques, his use of color and symbolism, his relationship to his actors and crew (whom he regards as "family"), and, of course, his own fame.

The most pervasive element in both his films and interviews is Almodóvar's relationship to the figure of the housewife who, in addition to being an ideal subject of melodrama is, he explains, "much more interesting as a social commentary." As one interviewer points out, "you are the only Spanish director who is constantly interested in women and their stories. The woman is always the protagonist in your films." Almodóvar's response is instructive for what it reveals about his personal preferences as an artist and writer, and his critical perception of his culture's social construction of gender:

> When it comes time to write and direct, women attract me much more. I've always liked feminine sensitivity and when I create a character it's much easier for me to do a feminine one, and I manage to shape it in a more solid and interesting way. On the other hand, women have more facets, they seem more like protagonist types. . . . We, men, are cut from the same cloth, while women hold a greater mystery inside, they have more nuances and a sensitivity that is more authentic.

This penchant for female subjects is reiterated in the 1990 *Cineaste* interview included here: "I'm becoming a specialist in women. I listen to their conversations in buses and subways. I show myself through them. For me, men are too inflexible. They are condemned to play their Spanish macho role." This is not to say that Almodóvar has absolutely disregarded male subjects in his films. His early exploration of what he calls the "male universe" in *Matador* and *Law of Desire* are, however, harsh and crude in comparison to his surprisingly moving portrayal, in *Live Flesh,* of the wheelchair-bound David and of Víctor, the "innocent" adolescent recently released from prison.

While Hollywood melodrama was very influential on Almodóvar's filmic exploration of the feminine universe and the expression of strong emotions, the interviews trace Almodóvar's transgression of his own generic and thematic boundaries. For example, in discussing *What Have I Done to Deserve This?*, he notes that the film is closer to neorealism than to melodrama. It also contains surrealist elements, as well as the absurdist and often black humor with which he colors all his films. As Marcia Pally remarks in her 1990 interview, this blend of neorealism with black humor is an element that links Almodóvar to other Spanish directors. While he likes to insist that his films are absolutely different from other Spanish and foreign films, and that this is the key to his international success, he nonetheless expresses enthusiasm for his compatriots, from Luis Buñuel and Carlos Saura, to Marco Ferreri, Fernando Fernán Gómez, Francisco Regueiro, Luis García Berlanga, Juan José Bigas Luna, and Victor Erice. But Almodóvar still laments, particularly in the early interviews, the fact that Spanish cinema has not kept up with the changes in Spanish society after Franco. "The gaze of the filmmaker is in the past, in the post-war period, and these are ghosts with which half the country cannot identify because we don't have them . . ." Perhaps in an effort to remedy this tendency, Almodóvar has began to oversee the production of films by a new generation of directors, through his own company, El Deseo S.A., established in 1987 with his brother Agustín.

As Almodóvar's cinematic style matures (and his success becomes recognized and assured), so does the tone of the interviews. All along, however, one retains the sense that it is a pleasure to interview him, even when, or because, he does not always finish his sentences, or digresses to a topic more of his liking. While all the interviews have a playful and informal quality, in the later interviews one senses a deeper engagement between Almodóvar and his interviewers. While remaining "exuberant, funny, and richly communicative as his work," as one of his interviewers put it in 1996, Almodóvar is nonetheless more intent on discussing his developing cinematic vocabulary and brand of politics. Increasingly, the interviews engage with questions of interpretation of the films. Almodóvar comes across as generously open to multiple readings. While discussing with Marsha Kinder the relationship of Pablo to patriarchal discourse in *Law of Desire*, Almodóvar explains that "those are new ideas to me, but I agree with them and find them interesting. I like to discover new explanations in my films."

While claiming to make movies that "deny the memory of Franco" and avoid overt political statements, Almodóvar concedes that with *What Have I Done to Deserve This?* his cinema starts becoming more tacitly political. In Celestine Bohlen's 1998 *New York Times* interview, he comments on the fact that all his films carry a political commentary. Exploring the lives of housewives is, for him, already a political statement in the same way that *Law of Desire*'s portrayal of a man's obsession to possess another man's soul can be taken as a tacit critique of the Franco regime. *Law of Desire* was attacked, however, not for its political metaphors which were overlooked, but for allegedly promoting homosexuality in the midst of the AIDS crisis. In defense of the film, Almodóvar argued that it was in part a response to "a kind of awful conservative morality that has developed since AIDS which is frightening and dangerous. . . . It seems to me that all the freedoms we have won can disappear very quickly. I feel I have a personal duty right now to be very radical in defending individuality above all."

Almodóvar's defense of individuality and freedom of expression has been the hallmark of all his films. He gives the disenfranchised a voice and a place, as well as control over their own destinies. While championing unorthodox desires, he is capable of generating empathy for his marginal characters. For example, in discussing his treatment of the Victoria Abril character in *High Heels*, he claims to have wanted to make a psychopath become a common person: "I wanted to explain the motivations and reasons that had pushed her to act in a certain way. Instead of detaching her character from the spectator, I try to make the spectator withhold judgment so that she does not have to be forgiven and the viewers can be moved when she is also moved, even while she does horrible things."

The tenderness and empathy that Almodóvar is capable of eliciting for the outcast and the marginalized is among the factors that earned him such an overwhelmingly positive reception of *All about My Mother*, winner of the 1999 Oscar for Best Foreign Language Film. The film represents a return to the street atmosphere of his earlier films and to many of his iconic characters: a pregnant HIV-infected nun, a single mother, a transsexual father, a dead son. As Guillermo Altares notes in an interview for *Positif*, "your films have always defended those who are at the margins, different; you have demonstrated that there is no good reason for society to pass judgments like perverse, degenerate, condemnable. For example, here you have a father with breasts . . ." Altares's comment creates an ideal opportunity for Almodóvar to lead the discussion in the direction of another of his favorite topics: the family. Here too, the director demands that his audience extend their empathy for and acceptance of those who have forged their own types of families out of an all-too-human need to belong. Families like his own, explains Almodóvar, with four children from the same parents who grow up together in the same town "is a concept that belongs to another age; the family has survived but has taken on a different shape."

Almodóvar's strong sense of his own individuality is palpable in the interviews and he defends it as much as that of his characters. He takes a certain delight in proclaiming his "talent for wackiness," his corrosive sense of humor, and even his fondness for bright colors and flashy outfits (he shows up for one of the early interviews wearing strawberry colored loafers and a red plastic briefcase). His free adaptations of novels into films like *Kika* and *Live Flesh*, or his unabashed appropriation (he even calls it "stealing") of Tennessee Williams's *Streetcar Named Desire* for *All about My Mother* and of Jean Cocteau's *The Human Voice* for *Law of Desire*, are the means through which he stamps his personality on the films and shows off his eclecticism. "I never cite a film as an homage or a quotation. I cite cinema as if the films I have seen were part of my life and of my experience," he explains in a 1992 interview for the Italian journal *Film Critica*. In discussing *Kika* in 1994, he restates the point: "You have to keep that original spark of energy, but not be faithful or literal."

The interview on *Kika* published in the 1994 spring issue of *Bomb Magazine* is among the most important ones in this volume. While it covers many of the same thematic concerns that surface elsewhere, it also indicates a turning point for Almodóvar. *Kika* is a film "which serves as a period, an ending to a chapter in my filmography which situates me in another one," he explains. The film is, by his own account, more pessimistic than his others. It reflects his own pessimism toward an increasingly mediated postmodern existence, one characterized by an absence of personal privacy and an overload of intimate details about other people's lives which, ultimately, lead to a greater, not lesser, sense of alienation in the individual. For him, all of this information about others with which we are constantly bombarded does not, paradoxically, lead to greater understanding, empathy, or solidarity. This is perhaps why Almodóvar's subsequent films become progressively more per-

sonal, warm, and imbued with a greater sense of humanity, and his inter-
viewing style calmer and more focused.

The impression one is left with after each interview is that Almodóvar's
commitment to individuality is less an irreverent gesture or a capricious dis-
regard for authority than a personal investment in assuring that there will
always be room, on and off screen, for the personal and the marginal. This
commitment to the personal also links him to other directors with whom he
shares, on the one hand, a certain marginality and, on the other, an international recognition and acclaim. He has been variously described as a Mediterranean Fassbinder, a Fassbinder with a sense of humor, a naïve and less
morbid David Lynch, as well as a "Woody Allen without the angst and Martin Scorsese without the guilt."

Cinema is, for him, a mode of personal expression, one in which he can
put his obsessions and problems on screen and have them reach a wide audience. Cinema is both the psychologist's couch and the priest's confessional.
It is also a means of rewriting the past, his own as well as that of his country.
"The difference between the dark past and now is that I am able to create a
future of my construction on film. It's a future that I decided to have." Film,
with a capital letter, is above all a "god," he says, his own personal god, the
one he has freely chosen to rule his life. When asked, "What kind of life do
you lead?", he replies: "One of work only, because with all of this about
being a 'self-made man,' I've had to dedicate all of my time to the profession,
and there's no room left over for anything else. My dear, this is like a priesthood; I'd love to enjoy an intense sex life and thousands of escapades but,
there you have me, totally surrendered to work."

Adhering to the policy of the University Press of Mississippi's series Conversations with Filmmakers, the interviews selected for inclusion in this volume have not been modified in any substantive way from their original
publications. As a result, a certain amount of repetition, and even inconsis-
tency at times, is to be expected. However, the very presence of such repeti-
tions serves to highlight Almodóvar's own thematic and stylistic continuities
from one film to another. Covering a period of twenty-one years, from 1981
to 2002, the interviews also reveal a maturing of the director's authorial per-
sona. As might be expected, the more recent interviews tend to be more substantive in relation to the films discussed. While the majority of the
interviews address multiple films and explore the intersections among them,
some focus more tightly on a single film.

An effort was also made to select interviews originally published in languages other than English so as to make them readily available to the English-speaking public. The first five interviews as well as two others later in the volume were originally published in Spanish journals, and I would especially like to acknowledge Linda M. Willem and Louise Detwiler for their translations. These interviews are particularly invaluable to the volume for the personal details they contain about Almodóvar's early life and career. I am also grateful to Cristina Degli-Esposti Reinert for her translation of the interview originally published in Italian in *Film Critica*. The translations from the French originally published in *Positif* are my own.

Finally, I would like to thank Peter Brunette, the general editor of the series, for suggesting Pedro Almodóvar as the focus of this volume, as well as Anne Stascavage and the University Press of Mississippi for their support and guidance through the process.

CHRONOLOGY

1951   Pedro Almodóvar Caballero, born on September 24 in Calzada de Calatrava, province of Ciudad Real, La Mancha, Spain (some sources list birth year as 1949 and date of birth as September 25). Father, Antonio Almodóvar, was a mule driver, bookkeeper, and gas station attendant. Mother, Francisca Caballero, appears in several of his films. Younger brother, Agustín Almodóvar, executive producer of their production company, El Deseo S.A., also appears in many of his films. He has two older sisters, María Jésus and Antonia.

1959   Family moves to Cáceres in the province of Extremadura. Completes elementary and high school education at the Salesian Fathers seminary and Franciscan Friars school. Becomes an accomplished choir soloist.

1967   Moves alone to Madrid after completing university entrance qualifying exams. Unable to attend the Official Film School which had been closed down in 1971 during the Franco regime, he makes a modest living as a "hippie" selling handicrafts (bracelets, beaded necklaces, etc.) on the streets at the Plaza de Santa Ana. Begins appearing as an extra in films and television programs featuring hippies.

1969   Goes to work for the Telefónica, the National Telephone Company for the next ten years as an administrative assistant. Joins the independent theater group, *Los Goliardos*. Starts to write comic strips and articles for underground magazines. Adopts the pseudonym Patty Diphusa and writes for *La luna*. Co-founder of the parodic punk-rock group Almodóvar y McNamara with drag artist and actor Fabio de Miguel (Fanny McNamara).

1972–80   Starts making Super-8 short silent films.

1974   *Film político; Dos putas, o historia de amor que termina en boda.*

1975   *El Sueño, o la estrella; La Caída de Sódoma; Homenaje; Blancor.*

1976   Trailer for *Who's Afraid of Virginia Woolf; Sea caritativo; Muerte en la carretera.*

1977   *Las tres ventajas de Ponte; Sexo va, sexo viene; Complementos.*

1978   *¡Folle . . . folle . . . fólleme Tim!; Salomé.*

1980   *Pepi, Luci, Bom, y otras chicas del montón*, first feature length film shot in 16 mm and blown up to 35 mm, based on the cartoon story about the punk movement. *General Erections* commissioned by the underground magazine, *Star*. Made for about $5,000 over the period of eighteen months on weekends. Shown at the San Sebastian Film Festival.

1982   *Laberinto de pasiones*. Score composed and performed by Almodóvar. Released in the United States in 1990.

1983   *Entre tinieblas*. First film to be shown at foreign film festivals in Venice and Miami and to be sold outside of Spain. Earns him international notoriety. Released in the United States in 1988.

1984   *¿Qué he hecho yo para merecer esto?* First commercial success in Spain. Released in the United States in 1985. International Critics Award, Mediterranean Film Festival. Palmera de Playa for Best Film, Mediterranean Film Festival. Best Film, Madrid Film Festival, 1985.

1985   *Tráiler para amantes de lo prohibido*. Medium-length film for TV.

1986   *Matador*. Shown at the Rio International Film Festival. Oporto Film Festival Awards: Best Film, Best Director, Best Actress (Julieta Serrano). The year's third largest grossing Spanish film. Released in the United States in 1988.

1987   Almodóvar and brother establish their production company, El Deseo S.A. Almodóvar is named Best New Director by the Spanish Ministry of Culture for *La Ley del deseo*, Spain's highest-grossing film that year. Winner of Best Feature at the Berlin International Film Festival, Premio Glauber Rocha for Best Director, Rio de Janeiro, and Long Play award for Best Director, Madrid.

1988   *Mujeres al borde de un ataque de nervios*. Goya Awards: Best Film, Best Screenplay, Best Actress (Carmen Maura), Best Supporting Actress (María Barranco); Best Editing. Best Foreign Film, British Academy Award. Goya Award Nominations: Best Director, Best Supporting Actor (Guillermo Montesinos), Best Production Manager, Best Photography, Best Art Direction, Best Costume Design, Best Makeup, Best Sound, Best Visual Effects, Best Hairstyle. Oscar nomination for Best Foreign Film.

1989   *¡Átame!* Goya Award nominations: Best Film, Best Original Screenplay, Best Original Music (Ennio Morricone), Best Actor (Antonio Banderas), Best Actress (Victoria Abril), Best Supporting Actor (Francisco Rabal), Best Supporting Actress, Best Production Manager, Best Photography, Best Editing, Best Art Direction, Best Costume Design, Best Makeup and Hairstyle, Best Sound.

1990   Wins the National Cinematography Award, Spain.

1991   *Tacones lejanos*. Best Foreign Film, César Awards, 1993. Golden Globe Nomination for Best Foreign Film. Goya Awards nominations: Best Supporting Actress (Cristina Marcos), Best Editing, Best Costume Design, Best Makeup and Hairstyle, Best Original Soundtrack.

1993   *Kika*. Goya Award for Best Lead Actress, 1994 (Verónica Forqué). Goya Awards nominations: Best Female Role (Verónica Forqué), Best Supporting Actress (Rossy de Palma), Best Production Execution, Best Art Direction, Best Wardrobe Design, Best Makeup and Hairstyle (Gregorio Ross and Jesús Moncusi), Best Sound, Best Special Effects.

1994   Named Officier des Arts et des Lettres by the French Ministry of Culture.

1995   *La Flor de mi secreto*. Oscar Nomination for Best Foreign Language
        Film. Goya Awards nominations: Best Director, Best Actress (Marisa
        Paredes), Best Female Role (Chus Lampreave and Rossy de Palma),
        Best Sound, Best Makeup and Hairstyle, Best Art Director.

1997   *Carne trémula*. Awards: Goya Award for Best Supporting Actor (José
        Sancho); Actor's Union Award for Best Supporting Actress (Pilar
        Bardem); Fotogramas de Plata Awards: Best Spanish Actress (Ángela
        Molina), Best Spanish Actor (Javier Bardem); El Mundo del País
        Vasco Awards: Best Original Soundtrack, Best Supporting Actor (Alex
        Angulo). Receives Order of Chevalier de la Legion d'Honneur at
        Cannes.

1999   *Todo sobre mi madre*. Awards: Oscar for Best Foreign Language Film.
        Best Director and Ecumenical Award, Cannes Film Festival. Best
        Director, Best Film, Best Editing, Best Lead Actress (Cecilia Roth),
        Best Original Score, Best Production Supervision, Best Sound, Goya
        Awards. Best Film in a Foreign Language, Golden Globe. César for
        Best Foreign Film. Best Foreign Film, British Independent Film
        Award. Best Film Not in the English Language, British Academy
        Award. Grand Prize, Cinema Brazil. Winner of 12th Annual Euro-
        pean Film Award, Berlin. Grand Prize for Best Film, Fipresci Interna-
        tional Critics Federation. French Academy grants him an Honorary
        César for lifetime achievement.
        Mother dies on September 10.

2002   *Hable con ella* opens in Madrid on March 15 and grosses $967,120 in
        the opening week. Loosely based on the true story of a woman who
        emerges from a coma, the rape of a cadaver, and the pregnancy of a
        coma patient. U.S. release by Sony Pictures Classics.

2003   *Hable con ella*. Award: Oscar for Best Original Screenplay.

FILMOGRAPHY

1974
FILM POLÍTICO
(Political Film)
4 minutes, Super-8

DOS PUTAS, O HISTORIA DE AMOR QUE TERMINA EN BODA
(Two Whores or Love Story Ending in a Wedding)
10 minutes, Super-8

1975
EL SUEÑO, O LA ESTRELLA
(The Dream or the Star)
12 minutes, Super-8

LA CAÍDA DE SÓDOMA
(The Fall of Sodom)
10 minutes, Super-8

HOMENAJE
(Homage)
10 minutes, Super-8

BLANCOR
(Whiteness)
5 minutes, Super-8

1976
HOMEMADE TRAILER FOR *WHO'S AFRAID OF VIRGINIA WOOLF?*
5 minutes, Super-8

SEA CARITATIVO
(Be Charitable)
5 minutes, Super-8

MUERTE EN LA CARRETERA
(Death on the Road)
Producer: Alicia Mora
Cinematography: Roberto Gómez
Editor: Julio Peña
Assistant director: Miguel Ángel Pérez Campos
Sound: Sebastián Cabezas
Cast: Paloma Hurtado, Juan Lombardero, Pepe Maya, Miguel Ángel Requejo,
Iván Villafranca, Carlos Villafranca
8 minutes, Super-8

1977
LAS TRES VENTAJAS DE PONTE
(The Three Advantages of Ponte)
5 minutes, Super-8

SEXO VA, SEXO VIENE
(Sex Comes, Sex Goes)
17 minutes, Super-8

COMPLEMENTOS
(Accessories)

1978
¡FOLLE . . . FOLLE . . . FÓLLEME TIM!
(Fuck, Fuck, Fuck Me Tim; Spanish title is also a play on the word "folletín")
Cast: Carmen Maura
90 minutes, Super-8

SALOMÉ
Cinematography: Luciano Berriatúa

Cast: Isabel Mestres, Fernando Hilbeck, Agustín Almodóvar
12 minutes, 16 mm

UN HOMBRE LLAMADO "FLOR DE OTOÑO"
(A Man Called Autumn Flower)
Director/writer: Pedro Olea
Cinematography: Fernando Arribas
Original music: Carmelo A. Bernaola
Cast: Francisco Algora, **Pedro Almodóvar**, Sonsoles Benedicto, Roberto
Camardiel, Carmen Carbonell, Luis Ciges, Antonio Corencia
100 minutes, 35 mm

TIEMPOS DE CONSTITUCIÓN
(Times of the Constitution)
Producer: Rafael Gordon Producciones
Production manager: Jesús San José
Director/writer: Rafael Gordon
Original songs: Fernando Brunet, Casaquemada, Luis Cobos, Pablo Moya
Cinematography: Miguel Ángel Martín Sánchez
Art direction: Augusto Brunet
Editor: José Luis F. Pacheco, Jesús Valdizán
Cast: Francisco Algora, Verónica Forqué, Héctor Alterio, José Bódalo, Kiti
Manver, José Cálvo, Alfonso Del Real, Victoria Hernán, David Thomson,
Pedro Almodóvar
101 minutes, 35 mm

1980
PEPI, LUCI, BOM, Y OTRAS CHICAS DEL MONTÓN
(Pepi, Luci, Bom, and Other Girls on the Heap)
Production company: Fígaro Films
Executive Producer: Félix Rotaeta
Producer: Pepón Coromina, Pastora Delgado, Ester Rambal
Director/writer: **Pedro Almodóvar**
Music: Little Nell, Alaska y los Pegamoides, The Ju-Jus, Maleni Castro, Monna
Bell, Tangos y Pasodobles
Cinematography: Paco Femenía
Editor: José Salcedo
Costume design: Manuela Camacho

Make up: Juan Luis Farsacc
Sound: Miguel Ángel Polo
Cast: Carmen Maura, Olvido Gara "Alaska," Eva Siva, Félix Rotaeta, Kiti Manver, Julieta Serrano, Concha Grégori, Cecilia Roth, Cristina Sánchez Pascual, McNamara, Diego Álvarez, Agustín Almodóvar
Cameos: José Luis Aguirre, Carlos Tristancho, Eusebio Lázaro, Asumpta Rodes, Blanca Sánchez, Pastora Delgado, Carlos Lapuente, Ricardo Franco, Jim Contreras, Cesepe, Ángela Fifa, Pedro Miralles, Enrique Naya, Juan Carrero, Tote Trenas, **Pedro Almodóvar**
80 minutes, 16 mm blown up to 35 mm

1982
LABERINTO DE PASIONES
(Labyrinth of Passions)
Production company: Alphaville S.A.
Producer: **Pedro Almodóvar**
Executive producer: José Luis Arroyo, Andrés Santana
Production Manager: Andrés Santana
Director/writer/production design/performer: **Pedro Almodóvar**
Writer: Terry Lennox
Painters and artists: Ouka Lele, Guillermo Pérez Villata, Costus, Pablo P. Mínguez, Javier P. Grueso, Carlos Berlanga, Fanny McNamara
Music: **Pedro Almodóvar**, Bernardo Bonezzi, Fanny McNamara; other music by Nino Rota ("La dolce vita" [F. Fellini 1960], "Rocco e i suoi fratelli" [L. Visconti. 1960])
Songs: "Suck It to Me" and "Gran Gagna" sung by **Pedro Almodóvar**
Cinematography: Ángel Luis Fernández
Editor: José Salcedo
Production design: Virginia Rubio
Costume design: Alfredo Caral, Marina Rodríguez
Make-up Artist: Fernando Pérez Sobrino, Beatriz Álvarez
Sound: Martin Müller
Cast: Cecilia Roth, Imanol Arias, Helga Liné, Antonio Banderas, Marta Fernández-Muro, Fernando Vivanco, Ofelia Angélica, Ángel Alcázar, Fanny McNamara, Luis Ciges, Concha Grégori, Cristina Sánchez Pascual, Agustín Almodóvar

Cameos: **Pedro Almodóvar**, Costus, Carlos García Berlanga, Ouka Lele, Pablo Pérez Mínguez, Guillermo Pérez Villalta
100 minutes, 35 mm

1983
ENTRE TINIEBLAS
(Dark Habits)
Production company: Tesauro S.A.
Producer: Luis Calvo
Production manager: Luis Briales, Antonio López, Tadeo Villalba
Director/writer: **Pedro Almodóvar**
Songs: "Salí porque Salí," "Díme," "Encadenados" by Sol Pilas
Music: Morris Albert, Curel Alonso, Carlos Arturo Eritz, Cam España
Cinematography: Ángel Luis Fernández
Editor: José Salcedo
Production design: Pin Morales, Román Arango
Costume design: Francis Montesinos, Teresa Nieto
Sound: Martin Müller, Armin Fausten
Cast: Cristina Sánchez Pascual, Julieta Serrano, Mary Carrillo, Marisa Paredes, Chus Lampreave, Carmen Maura, Lina Canalejas, Manuel Zarzo, Eva Siva, Antonio Banderas, Laura Cepeda, Marisa Tejada, Cecilia Roth, Concha Grégori, **Pedro Almodóvar**, Agustín Almodóvar
115 minutes, 35 mm

1984
¿QUÉ HE HECHO YO PARA MERECER ESTO?
(What Have I Done to Deserve This?)
Production company: Tesauro S.A., Kaktus Producciones Cinematográficas S.A.
Producer: Hervé Hachuel
Production manager: Luis Briales, Tadeo Villalba
Director/writer: **Pedro Almodóvar**
Songs: "La bien pagá" by Perello y Mostazo, sung by Miguel Molina; "Nur nicht aus Liebe Weinen" by Theo Mackeben, Hans Fritz Becmann, Wizner Boheme, sung by Sarah Leander
Music: Bernardo Bonezzi
Cinematography: Ángel Luis Fernández

Editor: José Salcedo
Production design: Pin Morales, Román Arango
Costume design: Cecilia Roth
Sound: Bernardo Menz
Cast: Carmen Maura, Ángel de Andrés López, Chus Lampreave, Juan Martínez, Miguel Ángel Herranz, Verónica Forqué, Kiti Manver, Luis Hostalot, Ryo Hiruma, Gonzalo Suárez, Amparo Soler Leal, Javier Gurruchaga, Jaime Chávarri, Katia Loritz, Francisca Caballero, Agustín Almodóvar, **Pedro Almodóvar** and Fanny McNamara (singing on TV)
102 minutes, 35 mm

1985
TRÁILER PARA AMANTES DE LO PROHIBIDO
Producer: Radio Televisión Española (RTVE)
Director/writer: **Pedro Almodóvar**
Assistant director: Rafael Moleón
Cast: Josele Román, Ángel Alcázar, Poch, Bibí Andersen, Sonia Hoffman

1986
MATADOR
Production company: Cia Iberoamericana de TV, S.A.
Executive producer: Andrés Vicente Gómez
Director/original screenplay/writer: **Pedro Almodóvar**
Writer: Jesús Ferrero
Songs: "Espérame en el cielo, corazón" sung by Mina
Music: Bernardo Bonezzi
Cinematography: Ángel Luis Fernández
Editor: José Salcedo
Art direction: Román Arango, José Morales, J. Mordes, Josep Rosell
Costume design: Antonio Alvarado, Ángela Arregui, Ángeles Boada, Humberto Cornejo, José María De Cossió, Francis Montesinos, Luis Ciges, Eva Siva, Jaime Chávarri, **Pedro Almodóvar**
Sound: Bernard Ortion
Music editor: Tino Azores
Cast: Assumpta Serna, Antonio Banderas, Nacho Martínez, Eva Cobo, Eusebio Poncela, Julieta Serrano, Chus Lampreave, Carmen Maura, Bibí Andersen, Verónica Forqué, Agustín Almodóvar
96 minutes, 35 mm

1987
LA LEY DEL DESEO
(The Law of Desire)
Production company: El Deseo S.A. and Lauren Films S.A.
Executive producer: Miguel Ángel Pérez Campos
Associate producer: Agustín Almodóvar
Director/writer: **Pedro Almodóvar**
Songs: "Lo dudo" sung by Los Panchos; "Ne me quitte pas" sung by Maisa
Matarazzo; "Guarda che luna," sung by Fred Bongusto; "Déjame recordar"
sung by Bola de Nieve; "Susan Get Down," "Voy a ser mamá," "Santanasa"
sung by **Pedro Almodóvar** and Fanny McNamara
Music: Bernardo Bonezzi, "Tango" by Igor Stravinsky; "Symphony No. 10"
by Dmitri Shostakovich
Cinematography: Ángel Luis Fernández
Editor: José Salcedo
Art direction: Javier Fernández
Costume design: José María de Cossío
Sound: James Willis
Cast: Eusebio Poncela, Carmen Maura, Antonio Banderas, Miguel Molina,
Manuela Velasco, Bibí Andersen, Fernando Guillén, Helga Liné, Nacho Martí-
nez, Germán Cobos, Maruchi León, Marta Fernández Muro, Fernando Guil-
lén Cuervo, Agustín Almodóvar
102 minutes, 35 mm

1988
MUJERES AL BORDE DE UN ATAQUE DE NERVIOS
(Women on the Verge of a Nervous Breakdown)
Production company: El Deseo S.A.
Executive producer: Agustín Almodóvar
Production manager: Esther García
Director/writer: **Pedro Almodóvar**
Songs: "Soy infeliz" sung by Lola Beltrán; "Puro teatro" sung by La Lupe
Music: Bernardo Bonezzi
Cinematography: José Luis Alcaine
Editor: José Salcedo
Art direction: Félix Murcia
Titles/graphic design: Studio Gatti

Costume design: José María de Cossío, Peris, Humberto Cornejo
Sound: Gilles Ortion
Cast: Carmen Maura, Antonio Banderas, Fernando Guillén, Julieta Serrano, María Barranco, Rossy de Palma, Kiti Manver, Loles León, Chus Lampreave, Guillermo Montesinos, Francisca Caballero, Agustín Almodóvar
95 minutes, 35 mm

1989
¡ÁTAME!
(Tie Me Up! Tie Me Down!)
Production company: El Deseo S.A.
Executive producer: Agustín Almodóvar
Producer: Enrique Posner
Production manager: Esther García
Director/writer: **Pedro Almodóvar**
Writer: Yuyi Beringola
Songs: ''Resistiré'' by Carlos Toro Montero and Manuel de la Calva Diego; ''Canción del alma'' by Los Coyotes, sung by Loles León; ''Celos'' by Jacob Grade; ''Satanasa'' by Fanny McNamara, **Pedro Almodóvar**, and Bernado Bonezzi
Music: Ennio Morricone
Cinematography: José Luis Alcaine
Editor: José Salcedo
Art direction: Ferrán Sánchez
Costume design: José María de Cossío, Peris
Sound: Goldstein and Steinberg S.A.
Cast: Victoria Abril, Antonio Banderas, Francisco Rabal, Loles León, Julieta Serrano, María Barranco, Rossy de Palma, Lola Cardona, Francisca Caballero, Agustín Almodóvar
101 minutes, 35 mm

1991
TACONES LEJANOS
(High Heels)
Production company: El Deseo S.A., CiBy 2000
Executive producer: Agustín Almodóvar
Production manager: Esther García

Director/writer: **Pedro Almodóvar**
Songs: "Piensa en mi," "Un año de amor" sung by Luz Casal; "Pecadora"
sung by Los Hermanos Rosario
Music: Ryuichi Sakamoto; "Solea," "Saeta" by Miles Davis; "Beyond My
Control," "A Final Request" by George Fenton
Cinematography: Alfredo Mayo
Editor: José Salcedo
Art direction: Studio Gati
Set decorator: Pierre-Louis Thévenet
Costume design: José María de Cossío
Sound: Jean-Paul Mugel
Cast: Victoria Abril, Marisa Paredes, Miguel Bosé, Féodor Atkine, Pedro Díez
del Corral, Bibí Andersen, Miriam Díaz Aroca, Nacho Martínez, Cristina Mar-
cos, Anna Lizaran, Rocío Muñoz, Mayrata O'Wisiedo, Agustín Almodóvar
113 minutes, 35 mm

MADONNA: TRUTH OR DARE
Production company: Boy Toy Productions, Miramax Films, Propaganda
Films
Producers: Jim Clawson, Lisa Hollingshead, Jay Roewe
Executive producer: Madonna
Director: Alek Keshishian
Cinematography: Christophe Lanzenberg, Robert Leacock, Doug Nichol,
Daniel Pearl, Toby Phillips, Marc Reshovsky
Editor: Barry Alexander Brown
Music editor: Bill Abbott
Cast: **Pedro Almodóvar**, Antonio Banderas, Warren Beatty, and a host of
other celebrities
114 minutes, 16 mm blown to 35 mm

1993
KIKA
Production company: El Deseo S.A., CiBy 2000
Executive producer: Agustín Almodóvar
Production manager: Esther García
Director/writer: **Pedro Almodóvar**
Songs: "Se nos rompió el amor" by Fernanda and Bernarda; "Luz de luna"
by Chavelas Vargas

Music: Danza española No.5 by Enrique Granados Campiña; "Concierto para bongó" by Pérez Prado; fragments from "Psycho" by Bernard Herrmann; "Youkalli Tango Habanera" by Kurt Weill; "La Cumparsita" by Matos Rodríguez
Cinematography: Alfredo Mayo
Editor: José Salcedo
Art direction: Javier Fernández, Alain Bainée, Cristina Mampaso, Nuria San Juan
Costume design: Jean-Paul Gaultier, José María de Cossío, Gianni Versace
Make up: Gregorio Ros
Sound: Jean-Paul Mugel
Cast: Verónica Forqué, Victoria Abril, Peter Coyote, Álex Casanovas, Rossy de Palma, Santiago Lajusticia, Anabel Alonso, Bibí Andersen, Jesús Bonilla, Karra Elejalde, Manual Bandera, Charo López, Francisca Caballero, Mónica Bardem, Joaquín Climent, Blanca Li, Claudia Aros, Francisca Caballero, Agustín Almodóvar, Carlos López Villanúa
112 minutes, 35 mm

ACCIÓN MUTANTE
(Mutant Action)
Production company: El Deseo S.A., CiBy 2000
Producer: **Pedro Almodóvar**, Agustín Almodóvar
Director/writer: Álex de la Iglesia
Writer: Jorge Guerricaechevarría
Original music: Def Con Dos
Cinematography: Carles Gusi
Editor: Pablo Blanco
Art direction: José Luis Arrizabalaga
Cast: Antonio Resines, Álex Angulo, Frédérique Feder, Juan Viadas, Karra Elejalde, Saturnino García, Fernando G. Cuervo, Jaime Blanch, Ion Gabella, Bibí Andersen, Rossy de Palma
95 minutes, 35 mm

1995
LA FLOR DE MI SECRETO
(The Flower of My Secret)
Production company: El Deseo S.A., CiBy 2000

Executive producer: Agustín Almodóvar
Production manager: Esther García
Director/writer: **Pedro Almodóvar**
Original score: Alberto Iglesias
Cinematography: Affonso Beato
Editor: José Salcedo
Art direction: Miguel López Pelegrín
Set design: Wolfgang Burmann
Costume design: Hugo Mezcua
Make up: Miguel López Pelegrín
Sound: Bernardo Menz
Cast: Marisa Paredes, Juan Echanove, Carmen Elías, Rossy de Palma, Chus Lampreave, Kiti Manver, Imanol Arias, Manuela Vargas, Joaquín Cortés
103 minutes, 35 mm

1996
MI NOMBRE ES SOMBRA
(My Name Is Shadow)
Production company: Ditirambo Films
Associate Producer: **Pedro Almodóvar**, Agustín Almodóvar
Director/writer: Gonzalo Suárez
Original music: Carles Cases
Cinematography: Javier G. Salmones
Editor: José Salcedo
Art direction: Wolfgang Burmann
Cast: Jean-Claude Adelin, Elena Mar Fernández, François-Eric Gendron, Fernando Hilbeck, Amparo Larrañaga, Nacho Martínez
90 minutes

1997
CARNE TRÉMULA
(Live Flesh)
Production company: El Deseo S.A., CiBy 2000
Executive producer: Agustín Almodóvar
Production Manager: Esther García
Director/writer: **Pedro Almodóvar**

Writers: Ray Loriga and Jorge Guerricaechevarría, based on the novel *Live Flesh* by Ruth Rendell
Music: Alberto Iglesias
Cinematography: Affonso Beato
Editor: José Salcedo
Set design: Antxón Gómez
Costume design: José María de Cossío
Sound: Bernardo Menz, J.A. Bermudez
Cast: Javier Bardem, Francesca Neri, Liberto Rabal, Ángela Molina, José Sancho, Penélope Cruz, Pilar Bardem, Álex Angulo
101 minutes, 35 mm

1999
TODO SOBRE MI MADRE
(All about My Mother)
Production company: El Deseo S.A., Renn Productions, France 2 Cinema
Executive producer: Agustín Almodóvar
Production Manager: Esther García
Director/writer: **Pedro Almodóvar**
Music: Alberto Iglesias
Cinematography: Affonso Beato
Editor: José Salcedo
Art direction: Antxón Gómez
Costume design: José María de Cossío, Sabine Daigeler
Sound: Miguel Rejas, José Antonio Bermúdez, Diego Garrido
Cast: Cecilia Roth, Marisa Paredes, Penélope Cruz, Candela Peña, Antonia San Juan, Rosa María Sardá, Toni Cantó, Eloy Azorín, Fernando Fernán Gómez, Fernando Guillén, Carlos Lozano, Agustín Almodóvar
105 minutes

2001
EL ESPINAZO DEL DIABLO
(The Devil's Backbone)
Production companies: Anhelo Producciones, Canal + España, El Deseo S.A., Good Machine, Sogepaq, Tequila Gang
Producer: **Pedro Almodóvar**
Executive producer: Agustín Almodóvar

Director/writer: Guillermo del Toro
Writer: Antonio Trashorras, David Muñoz
Original music: Javier Navarrete
Cinematography: Guillermo Navarro
Editor: Luis De La Madrid
Art direction: César Macarrón
Cast: Eduardo Noriega, Marisa Paredes, Federico Juppi, Íñigo Garcés, Fernando Tielve, Irene Visedo, Berta Ojea, Francisco Maestre, José Manuel Lorenzo, Junio Valverde
101 minutes, 35 mm

2002
HABLE CON ELLA
(Talk to Her)
Production company: El Deseo S.A.
Executive producer: Agustín Almodóvar
Director/writer: **Pedro Almodóvar**
Original music: Alberto Iglesias
Cinematography: Javier Aguirresarobe
Editor: José Salcedo
Art direction: Antxón Gómez
Cast: Javier Cámara, Darío Grandinetti, Rosario Flores, Leonor Watling, Geraldine Chaplin, Paz Vega, Fele Martínez, Mariola Fuentes, Chus Lampreave, José Sancho, Adolfo Fernández, Elena Anaya, Loles León, Agustín Almodóvar, Lola Dueñas, Ana Fernández, Fernando Guillén Cuervo, Marisa Paredes, Helio Pedregal, Cecilia Roth, Caetano Veloso, Roberto Álvarez
112 minutes

PEDRO ALMODÓVAR

INTERVIEWS

First Film: Pedro Almodóvar

JUAN I. FRANCIA AND JULIO PÉREZ PERUCHA / 1981

PEDRO ALMODÓVAR WAS BORN in 1951 in the province of Ciudad Real. Fascinated by cinema since his childhood, he attended a screening of *Gloria Mairena* by Juanita Reina (directed by Luis Lucía in 1954). He then discovered Super-8 cameras with which he began to shoot short films (*Two Whores or Love Story Ending in a Wedding*, 1974; *Homage*, 1975; *The Fall of Sodom*, 1975; *The Dream*, 1975, and the feature-length film *Fuck, Fuck, Fuck Me Tim*, 1978) and homemade trailers (one for *Who's Afraid of Virginia Woolf?*, 1975 and those grouped under the title *Accessories*, 1977). In 1978, he then made *Salomé*, now in 16 mm. He also began to shoot his first professional feature-length film in this format: *Pepi, Luci, Bom, and Other Girls on the Heap*, 1980.

Q: *Your films in Super 8 enjoy a certain, let's say, countercultural prestige. Did you set out to make them this way or were they simply a training ground for mastering the medium?*

A: The latter was implicit, but above all, what I wanted was to narrate in images the numerous stories that occurred to me, and that at times I expressed as short stories, depicting my friends at different parties. Regarding everything else, it's evident that those films have their own style, the kind of style that you're bound to adopt when you don't have any type of funding, that style that some call "spontaneous," the product of a language compelled by circumstances. And in light of these circumstances, the best that

From *Contracampo*, September 1981. Translated from Spanish by Louise Detwiler.

you can do is to try not to disguise them, like some of the "Super Eight-ist" people do, who pretend that their films are 35mm, which is a big mistake . . . In my Super 8 films, everything was used in terms of its own poverty, and this, inevitably, creates a style.

Q : *How did you manage to make* Pepi, Luci, Bom . . . ?

A : The story was born when some people from the *Star* magazine ask me to write a lewd and somewhat parodic story of the punk movement, sometime around 1977. Then the story began to grow and develop into a script . . . I had an absolute physical necessity to make the film because I liked the script a lot. And since I didn't have any funds, I had to improvise its production with small financial contributions from friends. The person responsible for knocking on the doors of acquaintances who could spare at least 15,000 pesetas was Félix Rotaeta, much more bold than I for these kinds of things. So, we reached a half a million and we could shoot half of the film, until we came to a standstill for a year. It was then that we got an executive producer, Pepón Corominas, who was better connected in the industry and supported distribution advances, and whose participation made the completion of the film possible. Needless to say, all of us who participated in the film, from the electrician to the main star, we worked as a team and, to this day (June of '81), they haven't paid us anything.

We shot the first forty minutes or so in June of 1979 and we didn't go back to shooting, except for a few scenes, until May–June of 1980. The final budget, including the transfer to 35mm, came close to eight million. I practically shot at a one to one ratio, and I constantly had to adapt to the lack of funding, which forced me to give up one sequence after another. And, I couldn't substitute fragments of previously shot material for sequences that a year later seemed more suitable to me.

Q : *Your film is articulated through diverse aspects of contemporary popular culture, filmlet, photonovel, gossip magazines, comics . . .*

A : That is a reflection of my taste. I'm particularly interested in those so-called "subgenres" . . . I think that the most important movies in the last five years of Spanish cinema are those of Agata Lys, María José Cantudo, Bárbara Rey . . . All of that is more interesting than what the serious boys are doing . . . Martínez Lázaro, Trueba, etc. On the other hand, in popular magazines like *Pronto, Vale,* and *Psssch* there is so much, perhaps unconscious, imagination, frenzy, and wackiness that makes for flavorful material which I use without altering it because it is extremely rich as it is. As for the filmlet, it appealed to me for its particular language. The ad that appears in my film plays with the contrast between a very careful and conventional image track (I even shot it in 35mm) and a text that is totally removed from what usually nourishes this type of image. I think that the world of advertising still has a lot of ground to cover to promote products in unusual ways, for example. Advertising, like "trailers," seems to me to be a very interesting way to make films . . . Detergent commercials, for example, seem very ingenious to me.

Q : *To what extent can your film be considered typical of a certain type of Madrid culture, also represented by specific urban rock groups?*
A : Some critics classify my film as folkloric. Others have seen it as a crystallization of the way of life of some new Madrid social groups. But the film is not an expression of any of that. I wrote the story in September of 1978 when the Madrid "new wave' didn't exist (although, yes, *Alaska and the Pegamoides* under the name *Caca de Luxe* did). What's going on is that those of my generation have been living "pop" with a certain parodic meaning for at least ten years. For example, Karina is the essence of "pop," which now would be "new wave." I've only taken some physical traits from this phenomenon so that it serves as a backdrop for me. But what interested me about the story was the female behavior, and some of the characters who, in any event, are not realistic transpositions, they are not trying to provoke identification nor recognition. I don't think that anyone can identify, as Carlos Boyero says, with Pepi, a girl who had to lose her virginity to a police officer so that he won't report her for growing a marijuana plant.

As for the rest, I don't know if the "new wave" boys would have liked the film, since they usually don't have a lot of imagination, they aren't witty at all, and they are well-off people. What interests me about the pop culture group is their lack of rebelliousness, their desire to enjoy themselves and enjoy life in the simplest way, direct and easy. They like to have a big pool, drink the best cocktails, and have the best clothing. And this can be analyzed from many points of view and can also be justified in many ways, but this phenomenon interests me more than the one about disenchanted people. Be that as it may, I think that the film is aggressive and the pop culture group is anything but aggressive. The film is somewhat subversive and inverts certain values, like the people, whose survival is observed ironically and skeptically, something that doesn't exist in the world of pop. In short, they are present as a phenomenon because they seem to me like the ideal subjects to give the film its shape . . . At any rate, my film does have something to do with pop. Its rhythm, its relationship to comic magazines, the stars of current pop that show up as extras (all members of *Radio Futura* or *Ejecutivos Agresivos*).

Q : *The fact that the protagonists of your films are women and the male characters end up being hurt ties your film to other recent works by Méndez-Leite, Pangua, etc.*
A : As you pointed out before, this is due as much to my interest in urban comedies—their universe is one of rock groups, policemen, and modern girls (good and bad)—as to certain kinds of feminine comedies, *Florida, Super Lili, Julieta Jones,* in which the protagonists, if they are secretaries, don't have anything else to worry about except for flirting with the boss.

Q : *In fact, the men who populate your films don't usually have well-defined dramatic functions.*
A : I write better for women than for men, who are dramatically boring to me. Additionally, I am better able to incorporate my talent for wackiness in female characters. I wanted to make a film about autonomous women, owners of their bodies and minds, who do without men, who make use of them . . . I did not want to make a feminist film either, but rather one that is outside morality.

Q : *Your film incorporates a new scatological dimension into Spanish cinema.*
A : Of course! Scatology is one of the new tendencies in sex, another element of the contemporary world, and its presence in the film is an expression of the reality that we must live. Scatology today, along with sadomasochism, is fashionable, like *parchesi* used to be in former days. In any case, it seemed necessary dramatically to integrate nasty things into the characters.

Q : *The character played by Kiti Manver caught our attention.*
A : She's a feminine character who was improvised, a trick that I used in the scrip. I like to fill sequences with people; at a certain point, between two successive scenes, I needed to establish a pause in the story. So I created a type of character whose narrative function interests me a lot. Cut off from the central story, this character can appear when it suits me. You wouldn't

believe it, but I was fascinated as much by the character as by the actress, so I went on; and as we went along, I was writing scenes that I would include when it seemed suitable to me. So, that's how she turned into a typical character whose story has been told in numerous photonovels.

Q: *She seems like an urban version of the character played by Sara Lezana in* The Strange Voyage.
A: Exactly. It's the same character.

Q: *Something else that caught our attention was the departure that your film makes from the usual characters of recent Spanish cinema, with whom it is easy to identify (educated professionals and the rest of the upwardly mobile yuppies), an example of which would be the* Ópera prima *by Trueba. Your film, on the other hand, is looking for other characters, is setting up other probable ones: people from the barrio, hoodlums, etc.*
A: It's a question of instinct. The world of the yuppies—which, by the way, must also have its charm, well, even the most abject worlds have it—neither interests nor stimulates me. If I want a heroine, I prefer a housewife, whose world is much more interesting as a social commentary as well as melodrama.

Q: *Regarding the formal carelessness of the film: is it the result of your production conditions or did you want it to appear as a stylistic trademark?*
A: I wanted to make the film, and I was even prepared to sacrifice it in the process. The price of making it was to accept doing without many things, some of them as essential as a good lighting technician. But I was not ready to let myself be overwhelmed by the difficulties, and in order to resolve them I adapted the tone of the film to these circumstances. It's poorly photographed, but I conceived a film in which the cinematography wasn't essential. In this sense, Arrebato would have been impossible for that film. That is to say, the technical shortcomings were not voluntarily chosen but rather had to be embraced. And even then, with the best camera operator, it never would have been a pretty film.

Q: *A film like yours, that breaks so much with standards of realism, likely characters, moral positions, etc., was it the target of any type of censorship, at the level of production or exhibition?*

A: The censorship at the screenings came after the premiere. In some of the old Castilian towns, the businessmen pulled the film the day after it premiered, under the pretext of immorality and poor taste on my part. Administrative censorship, as such, I haven't had to put up with any. Of course, I haven't received any prizes in the new talent category. I do, however, persevere and I'm preparing a film on Rheza Ciro's stay in Madrid, since he's been exiled to the most enjoyable city in the Western hemisphere.

Pedro Almodóvar: Life in a Bolero

MARUJA TORRES/1982

LAST YEAR, ABOUT TWELVE young filmmakers directed their first feature-length films. This is a truly unheard heroic deed in a country that continues to lack a film industry and where domestic motion pictures must survive opposite the incredibly tough competition posed by North American films. However, these young men—some of them now not so young—did the only thing they could to avoid drowning in desperation. They grabbed a camera, most of them 16mm that they later transferred to 35mm, and told their story. Often, their films are great. They are almost always extremely low budget, depressed products of the lousy quality imposed by funding limitations. But these films—put together during free hours on weekends, or in the afternoon, or after a day's work at the bank—are shot by friends who usually provide both the talent and the clothing for the characters, in addition to giving a flower vase after another for the set. These small achievements by impetuous movie-lovers who manage to carry their project forward, are, curiously, what enables one to believe that Spanish cinema is going to survive. Of course, that first endeavor is not always repeated. But, when it is, when one of these miraculous snipers persists simply because he has many things to say, one can argue that a film director is born. And, in this case, it's necessary to receive him with open arms, to welcome him into the circle of those who have nothing, if not an obsession to turn life into film.

From *Fotogramas & Video,* May 1982. Translated from Spanish by Louise Detwiler. Reprinted by permission of Fotogramas, Comunicación y Publicaciones, S.A.

Pedro Almodóvar is a significant example. From the Madrid "underground" and author of several absolutely shocking shorts and a feature-length Super 8, *Fuck, Fuck, Fuck Me Tim,* he debuted as a "serious" director—that is, with screenings in commercial theaters—with *Pepi, Luci, Bom, and Other Girls on the Heap,* shot in 16 mm and later blown up to 35. Now he's gotten Alphaville—the new production company—to finance his new film, and he's shooting it with so much joy that it's a pleasure to watch him.

A : We should put in the advertising: "Finally, a film by Pedro Almodóvar that you can see and hear." Because it's true. For the first time, I have decent funding and I can't believe it. Even the sound people are the same ones who work with Wim Wenders.

Q : *Whether living in poverty or not. Almodóvar is a born narrator and* Labyrinth of Passions, *his latest film, is a testament to that.*
A : My protagonists go through all sorts of things. Even the ex-empress Toraya (who is very annoyed by the history of this century because she is still in love with the Shah) participates (the film takes place when he was still alive in Contadora), and she comes to Madrid so that the best gynecologist in the world can treat her. My film has a thesis, you understand (and this is something I learned in film discussions, that you've got to have a thesis), and my thesis, which is the first thing I wrote, is that Madrid is the best of the best. Hell, in 1979 it was the gateway to the world. Now that the ex-empress can be a mother, she goes around like crazy asking for sperm from the Shah, who's too old for those kinds of things. But in the meantime, he finds out that the heir, Riza Niro, is there, and is not doing well at all in exile, and has been a nymphomaniac since the time of his most tender youth . . . and look how lovely, Riza Niro and the protagonist, who is a rock singer, fall in love and there is absolutely no sex between them. Well, she says that with him it has to be different, and by means of some typical misunderstanding between lovers . . .

Q : *He lets it out all at once, and if you didn't know him, you would wonder if he wasn't pulling your leg; but you know that Pedro Almodóvar is simply manipulating the material with which he nourishes his films: celebrity magazines, photonovels, the pop culture of serials cranked-up full volume, and the songs of La Piquer heard through the walls. Pedro Almodóvar came to the interview with all of the*

accoutrements of modern-day youth: Matching sweater and loafers the color of
strawberry candy, parachute pants like those in Howard Hawk's films, dark hair
cut in a disco style, and a red plastic briefcase in which he carries the script and his
notes. Pedro has dark and round eyes, lively eyes, like Betty Boop.

A: My fondness for genre films comes from being a spectator; I love watching them, and I'd like to make them all as well. It's just that I don't think
that I can. For example, I wouldn't know how to make horror films, I
wouldn't even know how to begin planning for them. I'm passionately fond
of melodramas, and in this sense I think that *Fuck, Fuck . . .* was very thorough because all sorts of things happened in it. I like atrocious melodramas,
like *The Step-Mother,* and not the embarrassing and disguised kinds, like
Kramer vs. Kramer. And it's just that . . . doesn't it seem to you that nothing
tells us more about life than a good bolero? Believe me, I'm not making this
up out of a love for the grotesque. It's the truth.

Q: *Pedro Almodóvar is thirty-two years old and from the Royal City. His father*
was one of the last muleteers from La Mancha, he transported wine to Jaén until
his mother—"who had a very strong character," Almodóvar emphasizes—got fed
up with that kind of precarious life and the family moved to Madrid. But, many
things happened before that: he earned his high school diploma, for example.

A: At that time, towards the end of the '50s and in my social class, it was a
privilege. What happened is that this must have shown that I liked other
things, and so my mother said, we've got to find something for this boy. And
since the only think that one could do then was to become a priest, my sister
(who was the oldest and had golden hands for sewing, and gave sewing
classes with the Lay Sister of the village) well, she spoke to her about me. The
Lay Sister thought that I would make a good priest and introduced me to the
scout in the area who looked for religious talent, and they put me in the
Salesian Fathers Catholic school.

Q: *So you began to study there.*

A: Actually, no. They discovered that I had an outstanding voice that could
reach something like eight octaves, and they turned me into a soloist. That's
how my career as a religious singer was started. Although I stopped studying,
they passed me in everything, like they do in American films with those who
excel in sports. In reality, although I was leaning towards becoming a priest,

it was the era for it, I was already sensing that it wasn't the modern thing to do.

Q : *And now? Do you sing?*
A : Oh, yes. There are two songs in the film, and I couldn't help myself, I put on the playback.

Q : *So, Pedro Almodóvar had a religious vocation?*
A : No, no, not at all. Between the ages of ten and twelve I went through a major nihilistic phase: life doesn't make sense, they brought you here and you don't know why. So, anyhow, when at the age of twelve I saw a film by Antonioni, I told myself, this man speaks about Life. Now I die laughing, of course. The tedium was the only authentic thing. And well, you already know that with nihilism you either kill yourself or you give it up; and so for nine months I imposed a religious fervor on myself; I told myself, okay, if this is true, well, it's close to me. But that didn't work either because, on the other hand, terrible things were happening to me. You already know what I mean . . .

Q : *They touched you? The priests?*
A : Yes, of course. What was happening between students was different, because you consent to it. But on the other hand . . . It was a shame, because sex should be discovered naturally, and not brutally, suddenly. For two or three years, I could not be alone, out of pure fear . . . I have never seen a place with more "mood," if you know what I mean, than the Catholic schools.

Q : *In this kind of climate, Pedro began writing, and one of his first stories was of a little lamb named Inmaculado. And poetry, in which he included words like "miasma" and things like that.*
A : Later, at seventeen, I came to Madrid and turned into a hippie because I saw that it was the most modern thing to do. I discovered drugs, alcohol, and Walt Whitman, and it took me a while to become a hippie, as long as it took for my hair to grow; but once it did, mine was among the longest. So there I was, with all those necklaces and glass beads that I made because I was penniless; when flower-power fashion came to the Corte Inglés depart-ment store, several directors decided to feature hippies in their films, and I

remember an amazing one in which I worked where the protagonist was divided between flamenco and *yeyé*, and in his dreams there was a group of hippies . . . well, there I was. There were just a few of us, who at that time were hanging out in the Santa Ana Plaza, and we made a living for ourselves as extras. And even Lazarov called us for television, and just as we arrived they offered us glass beads by the basketful and "put on whatever you like." And it was there that I learned the importance of costume jewelry. Later, I discovered that being a hippie was stupid, and since I wanted to study and I didn't have any money, I filled out an application to work at the Telefónica phone company and they hired me. That was in 1969, and since then I must have worked for a total of about five years, because I am always asking for time off; I'm actually taking some time off right now.

Q : *With survival assured and afternoons free, Almodóvar got wrapped up in film.*
A : I had a friend who had a Super-8 camera, and at that time they made what was called conceptual films, which is like having your back to the camera for an entire hour. I used to make narrative, and so now they don't put me in the catalogues; they say that I have not been "underground"; oh well, what can you do. The first thing I made was a story of a hooker who is pissed off because, with the liberalization of customs, she's left without clients; and then her fairy godmother appears . . . And, in the end, she gets married to another hooker and everyone loves each other and is happy.

Q : *Have you always been provocative?*
A : It shows a bit; it's not on purpose; it's just that I'm like that and I've seemed strange to people my entire life; it's just that here, in Madrid, I got more unnoticed since there are many here who are stranger than I. But if I do shock, it's in a spontaneous way; I don't have a calling for being scandalous. In *Pepi, Luci . . .* , I did include the pissing part and all that in order to scandalize; actually, it's introduced in a quite ordinary way, although perhaps this makes it worse . . . But, look, I saw myself as much more provocative at twenty than now; I continue to be spontaneous but I restrain myself in many respects; I don't have a whole lot of patience for the party scene, not because adventures excite me less, but because the possibilities for adventure are not real. Look, I love to talk to people, but later you meet a plumber and what he talks the best about is plumbing, and you end up not sticking your nose into a fascinating world. So, instead of talking, I've

decided to listen, and I go around listening; but because I'm a bit deaf in this ear, well, one day they're going to find out. You know, it's that Antonioni *was* right: communication does not work, there are magical moments, but generally it breaks down.

Q : *What nourishes your stories?*
A : Well, I read many things, and I love Virginia Woolf, naturally, but I would never turn *The Lighthouse* into a movie, just like I would never turn *The Aspern Papers* into a movie in spite of my enthusiasm for Henry James. The sources that have shaped me are popular ones. You know the amount of nonsense, of imagination, that are found in the lives of those people who appear in those widely published celebrity magazines—photonovels, radio theaters, women's advice columns—the people who all of a sudden ask what they have to do to firm up their muscles or cure asthma. My sister had a fashion design shop in Extremadura, and that world stayed with me, the world of the housewife, which both delights and horrifies me at the same time because its alienation is hideous. Yes, I'd like to make a serious movie about all of this; one could make a good argument in favor of housewives. But I enjoy its iconography a lot, and you could turn it around and use it in another way.

Q : *With that way of attacking that you have and with your past in the Salesian Catholic schools, hasn't it ever occurred to you to make a film about religion?*
A : Actually, the next one will be about these nuns who spend their days humiliating themselves nonstop, punishing themselves, and who dedicate their lives to redeeming girls who lead bad lives . . . and it has been very hard for me to recuperate religious elements, and it's because all of that is not in my life anymore, and it's a shame because religion can stir up many things in you, it enriches you. Buñuel would not be who he is if it weren't for Catholicism.

Q : *What are your plans?*
A : I don't make plans. Things seem to be going well; but I always think that they can go badly; this is from having been a poor kid, and that's why I ask for leave of absences at the Telefónica company; I'm never quitting there, just in case. It's like a kind of fatalism, a preservation instinct. Anyway, come what may, I will keep on telling my stories, whether it's by writing novellas or making films.

Q : *What do you think of the Spanish cinema that's being made now?*

A : You put me in a compromising position. On the one hand, shooting films is so hard, so arduous, that to make up for it you have to turn whoever does it into a god. But, of course, this doesn't mean that you have to like them all. I like the cinema of the older folks. Berlanga and Saura have been criticized a lot, but they're very good, even those of the generation immediately preceding mine are good, well, those who are seven or so years older than I, who are all burned out, like Zulueta, Ricardo Franco, Chávarri. But, right now, I'm not seeing the talent, the witticism, nor the power of these people anywhere among the new ones. A lot of folkloric cinema is made, which doesn't interest me, and the stories that they are telling us don't interest me. What's going on is that it's necessary to support Spanish cinema, whatever it might be, because you have to have a ton of poorly-made imperfect films, so that talent can surface. This would be resolved if there was an industry. Since there is none, we keep on being snipers.

Q : *What film would you like to make?*

A : A historical one. Like those from Juan de Orduña, but in another way. But I want to say that I would use all of the paraphernalia from Cifesa's works, and then that way, narrating, but doing it in another way, distorting it . . . I always remember how they used to tell me the story of "Juana the Crazy" in school; it used to start out, imagine, with her teaching her children how to sew because, she was telling them, before becoming a queen you have to learn how to manage a house. And then she pricks a finger, because she was so crazy, of course. Well, something like that.

Q : *What does your family think about your films?*

A : They don't watch them. My mother would die or something. In addition, she doesn't really understand at all that I'm a film director. After all, I never have any money. She only realizes it when they interview me on television and then, yes, I seem like somebody to her.

Q : *What kind of life do you lead?*

A : One of work only, because with all of this about being a "self-made man," I've had to dedicate all of my time to the profession, and there's no room left for anything else. My dear, this is like a priesthood; I'd love to enjoy an intense sex life and thousands of escapades, but, there you have me, totally surrendered to work.

And he takes off with his modern "look" and that elusive poet's halo of depilatory wax, epistolary romance, and home remedies for acne.

Interview with Pedro Almodóvar: *Dark Habits*

ANNA LLAURADÓ / 1983

AT THE LAST VENICE FILM FESTIVAL, he was called by a variety of names. For one sector of Italian critics he was a new Mediterranean Fassbinder or, better yet, a faithful heir of Pasolini's films. For others, his film was offensive, not serious at all, and even blasphemous. For most of the audience, it was simply one of the few unusual, fresh, and enjoyable films that were shown at the Venetian contest.

Dark Habits thus became a film scandal thanks to the morals and good manners of a well-intended Christian Democracy that did not allow the film to enter the festival. It was in this way that Pedro Almodóvar's third feature-length film embarked on its first international attempt outside of the festival. However, five nuns from the order of "The Humiliated Redeemers" did not need a prize for people to talk about them. With the help of their author, they went all around the festival surprising some, pleasing others, and scandalizing the more purist ones. And, as always, Pedro Almodóvar was making use of his imagination and wit in order to present a melodramatic story in which women—as usually happens in his stories—were the protagonists of a new narrative centered on a love relationship. After *Pepi, Luci, Bom, and Other Girls on the Heap* and *Labyrinth of Passions,* the young and multifaceted director from the Royal City abandoned the absurd for the sake of the absurd and the most excessive traits of the grotesque comedy in order *esperpento* to analyze and narrate his third story with greater calm.

From *Dirigido por,* October 1983. Translated from Spanish by Louise Detwiler. Reprinted by permission.

Gone are his origins as a film extra and employee of the Telefónica phone company. With *Dark Habits*, Almodóvar begins to get the hang of his narrative. Some of the elements that make up his style are repeated. Once again he uses a woman as the protagonist of his imaginative entanglements, and for the third time humor is filtered into the narrative for a surprising effect. But this time, Pedro Almodóvar breaks loose from the excesses of irrationality in order to submerge himself, armed with everyday things, into the most innately human emotions. Forty or fifty million pesetas and seven weeks of shooting, in addition to completely planning the story, have allowed him to mature and create with the camera. Whether one is in favor or against it, the result has been that *Dark Habits*—the third feature-length film in a long list of attempts in Super-8—has recently premiered on the Spanish screen.

Q : *Venice has been your first professional attempt on the international circuit. How did the possibility of participating in the festival come up?*
A : Well, in reality, it came out of my personal ambition. I had wanted to go outside of Spain. At first, I tried to do so with the Cannes Film Festival, but *Dark Habits* seemed too scandalous for them. The organizers didn't judge the quality of the film but rather its content and they thought that it had characteristics that they could not endorse. So, then, I opted for the Venice Festival, the second most important one. On the other hand, the film headquarters didn't have too many films to propose to the festival and they liked *Dark Habits* at the ministry. So it was finally selected, although from that point on problems began to arise. In Venice, some members of the committee thought that the film was great, they loved it; but there was another faction that was horrified by it, they found it anti-Catholic and blasphemous, and since the festival was dominated by the Christian Democracy—a somewhat short-sighted old school (he laughs)—the film was shown at Venice but not in the competition.

Q : *You've commented that when the film went to Venice the problems began and what is true is that the Italian critics branded you as a lousy director, your film as scandalous, and some characterized you as a new Mediterranean Fassbinder . . .*
A : I think that if the film is viewed from the point of view of provocation, it's not provocative in any sense of the word. *Dark Habits* is not provocative, nor was it ever, from its inception. I did not intend to be aggressive towards religious institutions; rather, I simply planned a love story. The Venetian

public, for example, was not shocked; they understood it and they didn't see any provocative elements that were not in the film. It's evident that there are people of all types, and there's no doubt that in Italy—where my cinema was not known and where Spanish cinema generally is very little known—the film surprised them.

Q : *But were you hoping for a reaction of such proportions?*
A : I wasn't hoping for anything, although I loved the public's reaction. On the other hand, there is the whole phenomenon of the media, which is very emphatic and sensationalistic in Italy.

Q : *You indicated that from its gestation* Dark Habits *was planned as a love story, but, why a story about and with nuns?*
A : Initially, I wanted to make a fairly "kitsch" film with nuns and songs, because I was enjoying the idea of it all; but once I began to write, I became more interested in the characters and I submerged myself into the lives of these nuns. In fact, the invention of the different universes in which they were living was appearing little by little in that story, which in the beginning was topical, familiar . . .

Q : *Nevertheless, your nuns are not very ordinary. What's true is that from the first moment a certain incoherence stands out in all of them and even more so in the mother superior (Julieta Serrano). Julieta's character is very sweet, maternal, spiritual, but at the same time she uses a whole series of material things—drugs, money—which seem to contradict her spirituality, don't you think?*
A : I think that Julieta's character is absolutely mystical, but the purpose of her mysticism is not God but other things, vices, if you will . . . Using a moral terminology, mysticism can be undertaken for any reason. Sartre used to say that Jean Genet was a type of saint and his saintliness consisted of helping thieves and collaborating with murderers . . . I think that a kind of inverse mysticism exists which is also caused by excessive love but which depends on the sensitivities of each person. And the mother superior in my story is a very mystical being, pious, but her piety is not directed towards God but towards delinquency. Piety, in fact, is the language between human beings and God but in this case God has disappeared and she substitutes him for delinquents.

Q: *God doesn't exist, but the attitude of the mother superior is Christian, which seems a bit contradictory . . .*
A: Yes, of course, Julieta's attitude in the film is absolutely Christian in the sense of protecting the helpless; not only protecting them but also transforming herself into one of them, which is the highest act of love and piety that one can achieve.

Q: *A Christian relationship without God . . . and God, where is he?*
A: He's not there.

Q: *Why?*
A: He has disappeared from their lives.

Q: *But your nuns wear habits, they have religious customs, they are clothed in symbolism, they live in a convent . . . so why all of this then?*
A: The truth is that I don't think that this is a contradiction of the story. The important thing for me was to talk about these religious women in whose lives God was absent, which is a way of being present. At one point, the Mother Superior needs God but he doesn't appear anywhere, and no matter how much she wants to become close to God once and for all—God, who decides the paths, who sets the standards—and she feels lost because this supreme being does not show himself, does not make himself noticed.

On the other hand, an autonomous process does exist in the convent, and it's when the mission of these "redeemers" stops working that they begin to spend their time on other things. From that point on we begin to discover their true personality, but they don't become aware of this reality and, because of inertia, they keep being nuns, continuing to identify with the life of the convent . . . But they move forward inside of themselves and when, at the end, when they must make a decision, they choose to follow their true nature.

Q: *On the other hand, in analyzing the film one would say that you don't have any ghosts. The need for harsh criticism doesn't exist. Rather, I would say that in addition to being a love story,* Dark Habits *offers a message of hope.*
A: Of course. In truth, I sometimes think: "I wish that nuns were like that!" And my spin on the film is not that "nuns are horrendous and it's necessary

to rip them apart," but instead I offer the possibility that they are the way that I'm presenting them.

Q: *Does your putting forth of this theme—lightly touching on the fact that Spain is caught between being mystical and grotesquely satiric, religious, and current—correspond perhaps to some kind of personal need?*

A: Naturally. Religion is an element that is closely tied to Spanish culture and although we, of the younger generation, worry much less about it, it's certainly still there. I suppose that it's because of all of this that I use it. Although I'm not a practicing Catholic, nor do I feel Catholic, religion is basically present in my life. And when I talk about God—present, absent, or necessary—I don't do it from a critical point of view because, additionally, I'd like for everything that's said about God as a solution to mankind's problems to be true. I don't believe in that, although it seems to me to be a marvelous invention.

Q: *Let's talk a bit about your narrative.* Dark Habits *gives the impression of being a more modern film than the earlier ones, it's more elaborate and even more tranquil, your way of narrating seems more peaceful . . .*

A: This is absolutely true. In fact, the entire film is made on the basis of very slow tracking shots. We move from one story to another, merging them, and the narrative is much more relaxed. It's also a much more thought-out film than *Pepi . . .* or *Labyrinth . . .* , with more rigorous planning and more distilled elements. And all of this happens simply because it's my third film and, inevitably, you learn as you go along. When I began to make films, I didn't know how to go about it—now either (he smiles)—although I basically believe that this isn't a drawback. Stories and ideas can flow even through a clumsy and rough style. On the other hand, I'm a person of action and I prefer to act now rather than wait for the perfect occasion, have all the funding, and have studied ten years in the U.S. In fact, I like my films the way they are. Truffaut used to say that the only way to make films is by making them, and however clumsy you might be, the technique is learned, the narrative film is learned, and now a certain kind of mastery exists in the third film. Also, in *Dark Habits* I had a higher budget—it cost twice as much as *Labyrinth of Passions*—and I was able to shoot it in seven weeks. All of this is noticeable.

But, aside from this purely technical aspect, it's also true that the story called for a specific narration, a more tranquil and relaxed style, more thorough, which basically has been a challenge.

Q : *On the other hand, one could also say that you've dared to investigate with the camera. The film contains a series of elaborate shots through which one can see your intention of discovering new cinematic elements.*
A : The truth is that for the first time I planned a film shot by shot. With the previous ones, I didn't take the risk of playing so much with the camera because the stories were complicated and the narrative had to be very linear in order to facilitate its comprehension.

Q : *Perhaps now you're looking not only for personal stories but also for your own cinematic narrative, one that is more creative than in the case of* Pepi . . . *or* Labyrinth?
A : *Pepi* . . . however clumsy, was a very coherent film. The coarseness and lack of funds with which it was created formed a part of the plot itself. It was the only thing that I could do. Of course, had I had more funding, I would have made it in a different way because as far as I'm concerned an aesthetic ambition already existed. But I didn't even have a camera operator and I had no other choice but to integrate that clumsiness into the style of the film. To this effect, *Pepi* was a product of circumstances, although I wouldn't want to go through that again. In fact, now I wouldn't do it again. Right now, I'm interested in fully controlling the technical aspect in order to forget about it later. My desire is to translate the imaginative talent that I have for creating stories and characters into cinematic language. But you can't do this if you don't have sufficient funding. And perhaps when I master it, I'll try to do something different, leaving the ''correct'' films behind. But you can't be a good abstract painter if you've never learned how to sketch first.

Q : *In your work, and I refer specifically to your three feature-length films, there are a number of constants, elements that are repeated, but* Dark Habits *has a certain kind of melodramatic air, the characters are more sentimental, they are of different ages, they live in another world, even if your norm of looking at them remains the same. In fact, it seems like a change in genre. What is your opinion about that?*
A : The elements that you point out in *Dark Habits*—which did not appear in other films—are substantially there and reflect the most obvious senti-

mentality, which I'm not ashamed to show. It certainly is a melodrama, although with a dose of humor; but it is a less corrosive king of humor, less wacky than in the case of *Pepi* . . . or *Labyrinth* . . . in which, additionally, feelings were not discussed. Therefore, I hope that the melodramatic element of *Dark Habits* is a new aspect, dealt with in a classical way.

Q : *On the other hand, another variant exists in your treatment of the absurd. In* Dark Habits *it doesn't appear as excessively as in the two previous films.*
A : Here it's more measured out, in effect. For example, the presence of the tiger in the convent is an almost surreal element along with the entire con-vent itself, in fact, because I doubt that nuns like the Humiliated Redeemers actually exist. But the play was different. Like always, I used irrational images, but on this occasion they are turned into everyday things, natural-ized like in the case of the tiger, of the drugs, or of the fact that one of the nuns might be a type of Corín Tellado. All of these aspects are dealt with in a likely way, which gives the story a different feel.

Q : *Nevertheless, the characters, their motivations, eccentricities, and passions do not seem completely defined in the movie. Except for the character of Julieta Ser-rano, the rest are rarely dealt with. Can this be understood as a weakness in the script or is it intentional?*
A : I think that in the film there is suggestive information instead of concrete data, although Julieta's role is, in effect, completely absorbing within the film. She's such a strong character that perhaps I should have made a film exclusively about her, because it's true that hers is the role that is explained the most and which generates the most interest from the beginning. On the other hand, I think that her portrayal is splendid, which gives her greater strength. Now then, I never create stories about one or two characters, I always surround them with secondary characters who at the same time have very powerful stories, but which for lack of time I could not develop.

Q : *You are perhaps the only Spanish director who is constantly interested in women and their stories. The woman is always the protagonist in your films. Is there a special motivation behind this?*
A : What you're pointing out is completely true. When the time comes to write and direct, women attract me much more. I've always liked feminine sensitivity and when I create a character it's much easier for me to do a femi-

nine one, and I manage to shape it in a more solid and interesting way. On the other hand, women have more facets, they seem more like protagonist types . . . We, men, are cut from the same cloth, while women hold a greater mystery inside, they have more nuances and a sensitivity that is more authentic. Really, I personally see more possibilities in a feminine role.

Q : *Women are constants in your film, but there are others, like drugs and homo-sexuality, which are also repeated, and which make you into a kind of chronicler of your time.*

A : I move inside a specific world in which I immerse myself and, naturally, I talk about it. Not with the exhaustive aim of saying: "I, witness of my time, I have to leave a legacy . . ." but, rather, I limit myself to talking about things that I see around me but without dealing with them as problems. Homosexu-ality, drugs, they're all there and I show them in a vivid way, but not with any intention of denouncing them.

Q : *What is true is that at a time when Spanish cinema is adapting literary works, theatrical works, and post-war stories for the screen, you are one of the few film-makers to show to us that our epoch, our '80s, can also generate stories of interest. Do you agree?*

A : Yes, completely, and in addition, our country is going through one of its most interesting moments and what's really missing is a narration of this period, it's for us directors to talk about this period.

On the other hand, there is the rise of a new mentality. The current change is so strong and concrete that I find it difficult to understand why it's not being talked about more. But as you say, the gaze of the filmmakers is in the past, in the post-war period, and these are ghosts with which half of the country cannot identify because we don't have them, and also because the last eight years are rich enough in events to be analyzed.

Q : *However, you analyze them with humor, you play with the entertainment. Haven't you thought about directing a drama or a serious story?*

A : Well, I believe that entertainment is basic to film; it's essential . . . Regard-ing the question of whether it interests me to make an authentic drama, I would hope, in fact, to explore all of the genres—although I don't know if I will be able to because the future of Spain is always a mystery . . . but I'd love to make a serious story. Unfortunately, I don't know if I will be capable of doing this since films inevitably reflect you, and my personality will always be present in my films. There is always humor in my life, an aspect that I perhaps use for decorum . . . (he reflects) and drama, yes, of course, in spite of the fact that it's very difficult to get people to cry.

Pedro Almodóvar: Cinema in Evolution

ENRIQUE ALBERICH AND LUIS
ALLER / 1984

N O O N E C A N D E N Y that Pedro Almodóvar's controversial film has, at the very least, one virtue: Its uniqueness. A virtue that, in itself, probably doesn't guarantee anything, but which is without a doubt the first step towards giving shape to all that is authentic, original, and unorthodox. These are words which acquire a renewed sense of importance in today's cinematic context, so ready to find shelter in certainties that end up later not performing as such. The forthcoming release of *What Have I Done to Deserve This?*—which was first featured at the Montréal Festival—his fourth professional feature-length film, offers *Dirigido por* a good opportunity to get in touch again with this production team.

Q : *For once we're respecting tradition and beginning with the customary question: How did the project of* What Have I Done . . . *come about and why did you choose the figure of a housewife?*
A : The truth is that I never know why I make one film and not another; it's something that I don't analyze beforehand, it comes to me in a way that is, let's say, visceral. When I'm writing a script I know if the story interests me sufficiently enough to go through all the trouble of looking for funding so I can then shoot it. If, in fact, the story stimulates me, it's a sign that I'm truly crazy about making it, and then I don't go over and over it in my mind anymore.

From *Dirigido por,* September 1984. Translated from Spanish by Louise Detwiler. Reprinted by permission.

This is exactly what happened in the case of my last film, except for the fact that making a film about a housewife has always appealed to me, since it seems to me to be a very rich dramatic premise. In the course of a day, a housewife has a wide range of experiences that could be tackled by any genre when you are dealing with this kind of a character. Additionally, there's the fact that I find the character in itself entertaining—even if the film has a dramatic background as well—and also that the housewife is a figure who is very linked to pop culture—a pervasive element that is in the minds of every-one at the time that such culture is born . . . it's not just during the time when I was growing up.

Q : *The film seems to take a middle of the road approach between various options. Well, on the one hand, it seems to rely on a very realistic treatment of things; but on the other, it introduces elements which are clearly fantastic, strange, and con-ventionally improbable, which emphasizes your distance from "psychology-ism."*
A : Okay, I take "probable" to mean that people believe what they are seeing and living, independently of realism. Probability in this film does not func-tion conventionally, it doesn't follow a naturalistic code . . .

Q : *Yes, this is very clear, and we believe that it's precisely when you most depart from realism that your film works best, and it even gives the impression that some-times you don't draw out the ultimate consequences of that very peculiar imagery that you have.*
A : It's odd, because while there are those who think that I should do with-out that extravagance, there are others, like you, who think that I should go even deeper into it. What happens is that I am not my own judge, nor do I try to defend myself against others; but it's that the extravagant element is always in my imagination and in my life and I'm not going to do without it. Why not put a telekinetic girl in the film? There are so many audiences and so many criteria that you can never find one that's representative . . .

Q : *In spite of this extravagance, however, the film gives the impression of a certain critical sociological intentionality, whose pertinence in relation to the rest does not end up being very clear. An example: the final sequences that progressively distance us from the protagonist's apartment, as if wanting to show that what we have just seen is a specific case in a great community of similar cases.*
A : It's also odd because I didn't do it intentionally, although it's true that,

yes, that interpretation, of seeing the protagonist as one more part of all of that, can be given to it. What I was really going for with the final scenes was the equivalent of a zooming away, abandoning the character and, therefore, the story. But, in any case, the fact that the story can be transcended and interpreted as you both have pointed out doesn't bother me. This kind of social element, which surely exists, is not an a priori intention, but I repeat that I don't mind that the film is being considered from this perspective as well. I really think that a political film has come out of me, one that almost resembles some of the neorealist films, although, of course, starting from different elements. And if there are people who are moved by seeing it, I believe that's because this film can provoke the same type of feelings that, let's say, *The Holy Innocents* can, but better and with more merit because, here, that emotion is obtained through more daring and purer elements, and not through specific cruelty, nor in a naturalistic or topical way, which is not as rich and at the same time is always the same . . .

Q : *Melodrama is a genre that is always latent in your films. When are you finally going to shoot an authentic genre, even if you subvert it, turn it around, or take it on as something excessive?*

A : I think that right now it's difficult to tackle a genre as such. It's already difficult to *believe* in a genre, to make it authentic. Inevitably, a distance, which in my opinion is insurmountable, exists between the genre and all of us. When you pick a genre, you do it purely as a stylistic choice. I think that what works best now is a mixture of genres, where each moment is planned as a function of the style that is best suited for it.

On the other hand, I love melodramas, especially the most outrageous ones. The Mexican Buñuel, for example, or those by Douglas Sirk, a marvelous director. But personally, I think that in making a decidedly melodramatic film there are two things that separate me from those who came before me, and especially Sirk: Morality—in all classic melodramas, there are the good guys and the bad guys—and humor. As I said, I admire Sirk's films, but one has to recognize that there is a complete absence of humor in his films. The humor that is there, is perhaps in the eyes of the one who sees it, but in no way is it the intention of the film.

In *Dark Habits*, yes, there is more melodrama than in my last film. In the latter what there is, is more drama, or tragicomedy. If I were to make a melodrama, I would come closer to the total surrealist excess that Buñuel used to practice and which some South Americans practice, or maybe I would tend more towards a much harsher "melo," the kind like *Leave Her to Heaven* or *The Main Thing Is to Love*—which it also is, although in another way, and it's very clear that Delerue's music fulfills a completely melodramatic function. The great advantage of melodrama is that it is a very open genre, in which you can put a lot of things and which you can approach in many different ways.

Q : *In your films, and* What Have I Done . . . *is exemplary in this respect, it seems that on occasion the humor tends to be a brilliant solution to a sequence whose mood was already failing, as if it were becoming a recourse, like a dramatic refuge, that at the same time operates as if you were censoring yourself, as if you didn't come to exploit certain situations until the end.*

A : Well, in order to discuss this we would have to review some specific examples. Of course, the film doesn't seem perfect to me; now then, don't both of you go asking me about films by everyone else because they seem like pure rubbish to me. When I critique my own work, I can find one thousand and one defects, and therefore I accept all of those that are attributed to me, but I also know, more or less, what good there is, as well as what good or bad there is in other films. It may seem pretentious to say this, but the truth is that I think that what I do is much more interesting.

As for the humor, I always use it, even in the most dramatic moments, and it's a direct effect of my spontaneity, which is precisely what sometimes shocks and surprises everyone else. I don't know if my humor, as both of you are saying, takes away from the intensity of a certain moment, but the fact is that my humor surfaces this way, spontaneously. When I contrast a dramatic situation with an enjoyable one that immediately follows it, I sense that maybe this humor ends up being disconcerting, which can give way to a fairly sinister effect, and I would love it if it could be this way. On the other hand, it's not very common for this harsh contrast to exist in film and it's very possible that it could provoke a sense of estrangement precisely because it's so unusual . . .

Q : *What is very evident is that from* Pepi, Luci, Bom . . . *until now, your directing style has evolved a lot. The sequence of the murder, for example, is very well executed visually . . .*

A : It's logical that it would be this way for the simple fact that when you advance in your career you learn as you go along. I'm very interested, in spite of what people say, in learning the technical aspect as I go along. However, what tends to happen to me is that, as a spectator, I don't pay a lot of attention to that aspect, and when I see a film that interests me I'm not worrying about where the camera is placed; rather I worry about the universe that they're showing me, which is what stays with me. As a spectator, I don't have an aesthetic bias, or a narrative one, or any of that. Now, then, as a filmmaker, I'm concerned with the narrative method and I'm interested in learning it, and learning it as soon as possible, above all in order to have more agility to manage the dramatic elements and shape them to my will more easily, like I can when I control the script. The moment I gain control of the cinematic narrative proper, I won't bother with the rules and all of that, but at least I'll have the reassurance of knowing that I'm familiar with and in control of the language, and that I use it as I please.

On the other hand, I don't want people to think that I make films without giving them much thought. Without having to reach very far back, in my last film I was very careful about the photography—I'd like to take this opportunity to praise Ángel Luis Fernández's work—and the lighting for each scene was planned out beforehand. With this I'm trying to emphasize that I do care about the technical aspects and the formal finishing touches. I think that the people who have attacked me by saying that I don't know how to make films are mistaken, and that this is the only argument that is not valid for attacking me because, among other reasons, there are a thousand ways to make a film. One does not always have to make *El Gatopardo*, for example, and I'm sure that when Godard made *À bout de souffle* that he didn't have much of an idea about technique either, but with his intuition, the strength of the story, and the characters he managed to make something that transcended any boundaries, which means that today, more than twenty years later, *À bout de souffle* continues to be a very modern film . . .

Q : *That's true, but nevertheless, it's a good idea not to forget that often it's the handling of the narrative technique that by itself arouses emotion and therefore makes possible that kind of communication with the spectator for which every filmmaker yearns . . .*

A : Yes, of course, I don't reject this technique in the slightest, and I'm wild about authentic virtuosos like Sirk or Hitchcock, and I'm wild about them precisely because they are virtuosos and because they show absolute control over the means that they have at their disposal. What happens is that, as I've told both of you already, I don't have any biases when it comes to cinema, whether I'm watching or making films, and that there can always be something that transcends the form, or that what people call "careless" is also an aesthetic option, a premeditated "form." I recognize, yes I do, that this is not the way to go and that, returning to the previous example, Godard could not have continued making *À bout de souffle* his entire lie, nor could I have continued making *Pepi, Luci, Bom . . .* , among other reasons because they converge with a series of circumstances, personal as well as production-based, which place conditions on you and force you to open yourself up to new perspectives.

Q : *We understand that you are already writing a new story . . .*
A : Yes, it's a story about two necrophiliacs, and I hope that it gives rise to a delirious, crazy, and unusual film.

Pedro Almodóvar: Grab the Fame and Run

ANGEL S. HARGUINDEY/1984

Q: What Have I Done to Deserve This?, *his fourth full-length film, is about to be premiered commercially in Spain. Almodóvar is once again on the attack, and he does so with a topic that turns out to be a familiar one in his filmography: the costumbristic and esperpentic comedy. From the most realistic details of popular kitsch surroundings to the most absurd situations. And with a clear preference for female characters: Carmen Maura, Verónica Forqué, Kiti Manver, and the always splendid Chus Lampreave add their strength to the display. Pedro Almodóvar is the George Cukor of the lumpen-proletariat. After his first feature-length film* Pepi, Luci, Bom, and Other Girls on the Heap, *he returns to the feminine comedy, perhaps with more wisdom.*

A: I think that with my latest film, compared to the first one, what attracts me the most is the character of Luci, the housewife, which is a character that I think can be the protagonist of any kind of film, from a thriller to a right-wing comedy. A housewife who is also a cleaning woman is witness to a great many universes. I find housewives very amusing, and I'm attracted to them. At any rate, *Pepi, Luci* . . . was what could be called a "pop" comedy, although with certain differences because it was corrosive and "pop" isn't, at least in its cimematography. My last film is dramatic. It's not even melodramatic. And it's much less comedic than *Pepi, Luci* . . . , and I've consciously left out all references to the "pop" world. It would have been much easier for me to make a comedy about housewives in the vein of *Polyester, Las que tienen que*

From *El País*, September 1984. Translated from Spanish by Linda. M. Willem. Reprinted by permission.

servir [*The Housemaids*], or Andy Warhol's *Bad,* or even some of Lester's films, something lighter. I suppose that I've changed a bit these last few years, but not much, and I'm attracted less to making something parodic like *Polyester* than to a film in which the housewife is present right there.

Q : *And already the initial problems understanding his language are there. To be present "right there," as the author calls it, doesn't have anything to do with the role that Carmen Maura plays or all the female cohorts who surround her. Sex under the shower, minislips, magdalenas, lizards, hams, mineral water, Nazis, frustrated writers, mentally unbalanced psychiatrists, murderers, telekinetic little girls, slot machines, the catalogue of things, characters, and situations that arise in* What Have I Done . . . *take us directly into the most multi-colored human market- place that can be imagined, but always within a consciously horrible aesthetic of self-survival. The reference to* Las que tienen que servir *leads us to talk about the Spanish comedy of the sixties, which was so reviled in its day, and which is becom- ing, with each new viewing, an anthropological document of the first magnitude.*
A : Look, I don't know if these films influenced mine in a conscious way, but what I do know is that they are present in my subconscious. Although it may seem pretentious, I think that all of those films of the sixties—*Los Tramposos [The Swindlers], Siempre es Domingo [It's Always Sunday], Las Chicas de la Cruz Roja [The Red Cross Girls], Margarita se llama mi amor [Margarita Is My Girl- friend's Name], Los Pobrecitos [Poor Little Things], Operación bikini [Operation Bikini],* etc.—were part of one of the most brilliant periods of Spanish cin- ema, and above all, they seem to me to be much better than similar films that are being made today.

Q : *The conversation now slowly moves toward memories, toward the early days of this filmmaker, and they arise spontaneously when the topic of how he is disliked is mentioned. Almodóvar, in addition to the quality of his work, is a film director who has managed to do something rather difficult in the business: to work continu- ously and constantly. Without having studied in any film school and without hav- ing been either a critic or part of a film society, he continues to make films, at least for now, at the rate of one per year. The answer to this mystery is simply his success at the box office. Nevertheless, Almodóvar isn't regarded highly by a good many of those who usually decide what is good and what is bad in cinematic art.*
A : It's clear that I bother many people, and not just the critics. It's clear because I notice it. I've received everything from anonymous threats on my

answering machine to some other things, but I'm already used to that because the same type of thing has happened to me since I was little. In my hometown, when I was eight years old, I didn't talk the way the other guys in town talked. I remember that in school I inspired the same rejection in most of my classmates that I now can inspire in the critics.

Q: *After clarifying that the town he is referring to, and the one in which he was born, is Calzada de Calatrava (Ciudad Real), the question "Why?" is a must.*
A: I wasn't a normal child, and fortunately that didn't traumatize me. I liked to read, which seemed odd. During recess I'd rather talk about Ava Gardner, for example, because even though I didn't know all that well who she was, I knew that she had had fifteen husbands, and that amused me more than playing.

Q: *What school was that?*
A: A Franciscan school in Cáceres. For financial reasons my family moved from Ciudad Real to Madrigalejo in Cáceres, and I studied for my bachillerato [equivalent of junior college] degree, in boarding school.

Q: *You studied for your bachillerato in Cáceres, and did you then come to Madrid with your whole family?*
A: When I reached the age of sixteen, upon completing my bachillerato, my father decided that I should go to work in an office in Madrigalejo, and I told him no way, that I was going to Madrid to try to continue to study and work. I came to a small apartment that my parents had bought, so at least I was assured of having a roof over my head, and I got to know the city.

Q: *It's a typical cinematic story: young man from the provinces arrives in the big city with the will to succeed. It's like a musical in which, instead of Fred Astaire, this protagonist buys himself a thick robe and house slippers and acts, with musical accompaniment, in front of the elite of modernity. The setting and the styles change, but the story stays the same. In the case of Pedro Almodóvar, even life and cinema coincide in a happy ending: small town boy makes good.*
A: When I arrived, I realized that continuing my studies was going to be hard to do. I went to the Plaza de Santa Ana—I'm talking about 1967—and I started to make beaded necklaces, bracelets, and all of the hippie paraphernalia. I had it all covered, even to the last detail of going to Ibiza. A year later I

got beyond that because I was already getting bored. I was looking for something more sophisticated.

Q : *And had you already linked up with the theatrical group, Los Goliardos?*
A : Yes, I joined Los Goliardos and simultaneously began working for the telephone company, because I had taken the exam to be an administrative assistant, and they passed me. Well, the truth is that my entrance into the telephone company was quite spectacular. I had very long hair and for the photos and the exams I gathered it up with hairpins and stuck it under my shirt. When they passed me and I went to introduce myself, I let my hair out, which gave the section chief a heart attack, and he said that he wouldn't let anyone in who looked like that. I arrived at my post and I realized that something strange was going on because they didn't assign me any table. They just had me sit in a type of waiting room. Soon afterwards I found out that all of the section chiefs at the plant had gotten together to decide what to do with me, because they couldn't throw me out without allowing me to work first. And my chief refused to have me work with him. Fortunately, there was a chief who was a bit more modern and he said, "Well, I'll take him." At the same time that I began to work at the telephone company I met various people, like Félix Rotaeta, who put me in contact with Los Goliardos when the group was a bit down on its luck. I worked at mounting some plays, like *Don Juan,* which never was performed. And along with Ignacio Gómez de Liaño, Herminio Molero, and others, I did some "happenings" in art galleries. That was in 1969 and 1970.

Q : *From this hippie phase to the artistic vanguard, there is a coherent evolution which, surprisingly perhaps, manages to confirm one of the current sources of inspiration for this prolific auteur: the advice to the lovelorn column in the magazine* Pronto.
A : Well, it's true. I'd say that if you want an edifying and entertaining column to read, that's the one. More than that, I think that there's more of a sense of humor and a greater capacity for surprise in *Pronto* than in many of today's Spanish novels.

Q : *Which doesn't keep you from also being interested in other authors.*
A : Well, sure, of course. I'm very interested in people like Ramón Gómez de la Serna, Mihura, Edgar Neville, etc., who also are not very original, although

they are absolutely Spanish. As a reader I have a very wide range, as wide as my range as a viewer. In the latter case, I can enjoy anything from second-rate terror films—like *El Día de la madre [Mother's Day]* or *Trampa mortal [Death Trap]*, which excite me as much as more sophisticated films like *American Gigolo*—to any of Wender's films. I have a good time with all genres. And it's the same with literature. I read the novels of Corín Tellado, or I allow myself to be fascinated by people like Jane Bowles, or Faulkner, or Flaubert. That is, I go from one end of the spectrum to the other.

Q: *You arrive at "professional" cinema, in quotes, with* Pepi, Luci . . . *after a lengthy period in Super-8.*
A: Really, *Pepi, Luci . . .* was done in the very same manner as a Super-8 film, not only from a formal or narrative point of view, but also from that of the production stage, if it can be called production. Well, it went like this: Félix Rotaeta and Carmen Maura said that the story should be filmed in a better format than Super-8, and Félix began to tap all of his friends for money. When we had some money, we would call up friends and film whatever we could in their homes. It took us a year and a half to finish it.

Q: *Then* Pepi, Luci . . . *premiered and success arrived, especially as measured from a financial point of view: the costs were significantly less than the box office receipts. In the first place, it was a box office success, and gave you the possibility to continue making films. And along with success came the popularity, the interviews, the television, and all of that. Was that world of success and popularity the world you had in mind when you were young even though you weren't familiar with it?*
A: In principle, success is very pleasant, and since I like to experience everything, I craved it. I had a good time with the interviews, etc. But it wasn't the world of success itself that I yearned for. I could have been interested in the world of success that Georges Miller has, whose entire staff is behind him to protect him, to solve his problems, to put itself out for him. But since in Spain success translates into being invited to lots of parties, having lots of interviews, and appearing in lots of magazines, that really wasn't what I had dreamed of because it isn't all that much fun. The extent to which it does coincide with what I had imagined is that it allows me to work in a medium like film and make a living from it.

Q : *Another of your creative outlets is literature or journalistic collaborations. I'm thinking now about the memoirs of Patty Diphusa, or that short novel* Fuego en las entrañas [Fire in the Belly] *with Mariscal's sketches. Everything seems to indicate that film is keeping you from continuing to write.*

A : That's something that interests me a lot. It's not that I think that I have exceptional talent, but I do write well enough to be published, which I think is sufficient. The realm of literature is something that I'm always putting off for when I have more time, because I do want to write novels, especially like now when I read a novel like *Wilt* by Tom Sharpe, which I don't think I could have written but I would have liked to have written. And while I can't write like Henry Miller, for example, I do think that I might be able to approach the style of Sharpe. It makes me very envious and it's an area in which I'm always falling behind.

Q : *We're now entering into the smallest realm of your artistic activity, although it's not any less known: your public concerts in collaboration with Fabio de Miguel.*

A : I enjoy it very, very much. I enjoy doing it every once in a while, because they have invited us to lots of places and we can't go to them all. What I don't like—and I'll give Divine as an example—is to be under contract and to travel all over doing more or less the same thing at all the concerts. That isn't enjoyable at all to me. I, for example, go out in a thick woman's housecoat. First, there's something that no one ends up believing, and that's that I act completely naturally according to the moment. That is, at the time I didn't have money to buy a super glitter outfit, which I would have loved. Something like Imagination or Bonny M. But I never had either the money nor the time, so I went to the store Almacenes Arias and with 1,000 pesetas I put together the entire outfit: tasseled slippers, thick robe, and women's underwear. That, then, is lots of fun, because, in my case, it's titillating to see a film director go out on stage like a bitch.

Q : *In his latest film,* What Have I Done . . . *the director, along with Fabio de Miguel, perform* La bien pagá [The Well-Paid Woman] *dressed, respectively, as a hussar and a cross between Eugenia de Montijo and Scarlet O'Hara, which definitively erases the image of a housewife in tasseled slippers. This new change of image will go along with a new change of theme in his next film, which he is working on now and in which eroticism and violent death are closely linked. Almodóvar names the two directors he most admires: Luis Buñuel (especially during his Mexican period, for doing all that he did with the resources he was given) and Orson Welles (whom Almodóvar recognizes as being farther removed from him due to his culture, restlessness, etc.) And the last part of our conversation can't be anything other than about love, particularly with a director for whom emotional relationships, regardless of sexual distinctions, are basic to his feature-length films. Could we talk about love?*

A : We haven't talked about love, that's true. I'm a rather passionate person.

Q : *And one who falls in love easily?*
A : No, no, I'm not easily infatuated. Although it seems a bit pretentious, one of the constants in my life has been a type of dissatisfaction. Although it doesn't keep me from enjoying anything—I intensely enjoy everything I do—I always have the feeling that it could have been better. I think that love brings out the worst in me. I begin to notice that I'm in love at the same time that I begin to lose my sense of humor, which is a terrifying thing. On the other hand, since my profession is to make films and literature, and I want all of it to exude life, I decided that I can't live a life of abstinence in the emotional realm. I opened my doors and put myself out there. For a year now I've been the most accessible guy in the city in that way—physically— and it's curious because from the moment that you put yourself out there, people sense it and lots of things start to happen to you.

Q : *Who was your first love?*
A : My first love was in school, in Cáceres, something very much out of the movies.

Q : *A movie by Summers?*
A : No, not a movie by Summers, but rather, one like those with Katharine Hepburn and Cary Grant.

Q : *Not like the ones with Judy Garland and Mickey Rooney.*
A : Ha, ha, ha. Yes, those with Mickey Rooney and Judy Garland. Well, at any rate, in our case we were both either Cary Grant or Mickey Rooney. I was the insufferable star at school; the one that did everything well and was the luckiest in his studies. The other boy was the complete opposite. He was the kinkiest guy at school and the one who played better at everything. I was at the head of the group of perfect students, and he was at the head of the

biggest goof-offs. We were two people who stuck out from the rest, and I suppose that we were bound to find each other.

Q : *Do you have some kind of unrealized erotic fantasy?*
A : Well, yes. My erotic fantasy is to go on a bus, to pass by a school, and to see, for example, a father of about thirty-eight picking up his thirteen year old daughter. What I would really like is to go to bed with the father and the daughter at the same time, because I like pubescents a lot, and their fathers, even those with respectable jobs that give them a bit of a paunch.

Q : *Thirty-four years of age, from the country to the city, from the telephone company to stardom, from absurd costumbristic comedies to reflections on love and death, from pubescent daughters to fathers who are dentists or lawyers, Pedro Almodóvar survives in the urban jungle with talent and courage. He knows that success isn't forgiven but he doesn't care. Some day he will have a chalet with a pool and he will throw the best parties in the city while his detractors argue about the latest Bresson over a cup of coffee.*

Pleasure and the New Spanish Mentality: A Conversation with Pedro Almodóvar*

MARSHA KINDER/1987

FOLLOWING THE ENTHUSIASTIC critical reception of Pedro Almodóvar's *La Ley del deseo (The Law of Desire)* at this year's Berlin Film Festival, Spain's oldest and largest-circulation film journal, *Fotogramas & Video,* ran an editorial saying:

> The recent Berlin Festival has demonstrated an important fact for Spanish cinema: the interest that our cinema can arouse abroad, not only at the level of interchange or cultural curiosity, but as an exportable and commercially valid product. . . . Spanish cinema is trying to leave the national "ghetto" and join a movement that proclaims the necessity and urgency of a "European cinema" which transcends nationalities without renouncing their specificity.[1]

Although this editorial mentions several films at the festival to support its point, it focuses most specifically on "the enormous and overwhelming success of *La Ley del deseo* . . . , a film that is eminently 'Spanish' but comprehensible to any person," and which confirms that "when one makes a cinema that has something to say, these things can have appeal everywhere."

From *Film Quarterly,* vol. 41, no. 1 (Fall 1987): pp. 33–44. Copyright © 1987 by The Regents of the University of California. Reprinted by permission of *Film Quarterly* and the author.
*This conversation took place on May 25, 1987 at Pedro Almodóvar's piso in Madrid. It was made possible by a research grant from the Comité Conjunto Hispano Norteamericano para la Cooperación Cultural y Educativa.
[1] "Cine Español: De Lo Particular a lo Universal," *Fotogramas & Video* (April 1987), p. 7. The translation to English is mine.

Fotogramas fails to acknowledge the irony that this film being singled out as a model of "universal" appeal is an outrageous melodrama featuring homosexual and transsexual protagonists in a sadomasochistic triangle involving incest, murder, and suicide and including several sexually explicit homoerotic love scenes. It's a film that in most national contexts would be marginal, to say the least. And yet in March, when it was screened in New York, concurrent with but not as part of the Ministry of Culture's Third Annual Spanish Film Week (which included an equally extreme Almodóvar melodrama called *Matador*), *La Ley del deseo* again received critical raves in the *Village Voice* and in the *New Yorker* where Pauline Kael devoted a full page to the film—an achievement that was duly reported as "news" in Spain's most prestigious daily, *El País*.[2]

At the very moment when Spanish cinema may be facing its most serious economic crisis, Almodóvar's films are achieving modest success both at home and abroad. Since the death of Franco in 1975 and despite the earnest efforts of the Socialist government which came to power in 1982, Spanish films have not only failed to find adequate distribution in foreign markets, but they have steadily been losing their home audience. Spanish spectators are either staying home in droves with their VCRs or flocking to see the latest imports which increasingly dominate Spanish movie houses with their block booking. The number of total spectators who attended movies in Spain decreased from 331 million in 1970 to 101 million in 1985, and by 1985 Spanish films held only 17.5 percent of that diminishing home market, as opposed to 30 percent in 1970.[3] Within this discouraging context, Almodóvar's early features did surprisingly well in Spain and *Matador* was an outstanding success—the third-largest-grossing Spanish film in 1986.[4] The final figures are not yet in on *La Ley del deseo,* but they promise to be even better. It's the first Almodóvar film to be immediately sold worldwide—virtually everywhere but in Japan.

Almodóvar's films have a curious way of resisting marginalization. Never limiting himself to a single protagonist, he chooses an ensemble of homosex-

---

[2] Pauline Kael, "Manypeeplia Upsidownia," *The New Yorker* (April 20, 1987).

[3] Javier Castro, "20 Años de Mercado Cinematográfico Español," *Cineinforme,* Edicion Especial, No 494 (Septiembre 1986), pp. 70–71.

[4] Francisco Llinas, *4 Años de Cine Español* (1983–86). Madrid: Festival Internacional de Madrid, IMAGFIC, 1987, p. 99.

ual, bisexual, transsexual, doper, punk, terrorist characters who refuse to be ghettoized into divisive subcultures because they are figured as part of the "new Spanish mentality"—a fast-paced revolt that relentlessly pursues pleasure rather than power, and a post-modern erasure of all repressive boundaries and taboos associated with Spain's medieval, fascist, and modernist heritage. Almodóvar claims:

> I always try to choose prototypes and characters from modern-day Madrid, who are somehow representative of a certain mentality existing today. . . . I think that since Franco died new generations have been coming to the fore, generations that are unrelated to former ones, that are even unrelated to the "progressive" generations that appeared during the last years of the dictatorship. How do people twenty years old live in Madrid? It's quite complex. . . . The characters in my films utterly break with the past, which is to say that most of them, for example, are apolitical. Pleasure must be grasped immediately, hedonistically; that is almost the main leitmotif of their lives.[5]

This new mentality was already present in Almodóvar's first low-budget, underground feature (made in 16mm and blown up to 35), *Pepi, Luci, Bom y Otras Chicas del Montón* (retitled in English *Pepi, Luci, Bom and Other Girls on the Heap,* 1980), where a policeman, who's married to middle-aged Luci, rapes their young neighbor Pepi and tries to cover up his crime by planting marijuana on her balcony. Luci responds by becoming sexually involved with a girl even younger than Pepi, a sixteen-year-old pleasure lover named Bom, and Pepi writes their love story. The rape is further avenged by Pepi's friends from a punk rock group who, in order to attract the rapist, disguise themselves as traditional Spanish zarzuela singers.

The new mentality of twenty-year-olds was seen even more clearly in Almodóvar's second splashy feature *Laberinto de pasiones* (*Labyrinth of Passions,* 1982), which positively bristles with vibrant color and a wildly comic sexual energy. The tortuously complex plot follows the tangled passions of an ensemble of young Madrileños trying to escape the crippling influences of repressive fathers in order to pursue their own pleasure. Riza Niro (Imanol Arias) is the bisexual son of the deposed "emperor of Tehran." More inter-

---

[5] Quoted by Peter Besas in *Behind the Spanish Lens: Spanish Cinema under Fascism and Democracy.* Denver: Arden Press, 1985, p. 216.

ested in sex and cosmetics than in family or politics, he flees his corrupt, cancerous father and lecherous, infertile stepmother, becomes a punk singer in Madrid, and ultimately flies away with the Felliniesque Sexilia (Celia Roth), a nymphomaniac member of a feminist punk band called "Las Ex" and daughter of a world-class sex-loathing gynecologist, whose scientific detachment drives his daughter to promiscuity. Queti, a young laundress who is chronically raped by her dry-cleaning daddy on alternate days, undergoes plastic surgery to become Sexilia's surrogate on stage and at home where she enters a budding incestuous relationship with her new doctor daddy. This two-faced incestuous daughter feeds both daddies powerful potions that render one impotent, the other horny. The fleeing lovers Riza and Sexy are hotly pursued by an assortment of jealous punks and Islamic fundamentalists, but none so dogged as the super-keen-scented Sadec, a handsome Tehranian terrorist (played by Antonio Banderas) who also loves Riza in spite of politics. This "musical comedy" (for which Almodóvar himself wrote and performed some of the wildest songs) is still running on weekends as a midnight cult movie in Madrid.

Though I haven't seen Almodóvar's third feature, *Entre tinieblas* (retitled in English *Dark Habits*, 1983), it's reported to be about a community of nuns known as the "Humble Redeemers" who run a home for delinquent girls, where, among other pleasurable pastimes, the sisters keep a pet tiger, write steamy best-sellers, smoke pot, and shoot dope.

¿Qué he hecho yo para merecer ésto? (What Have I Done to Deserve This?, 1984/85), Almodóvar's first international hit, follows the travails of Gloria (Carmen Maura), a high-rise suburban housewife who toils as a maid to help support her family, which includes: a taxi-driver husband who's obsessed with a suicidal German singer and who gets involved in a plot to forge Hitler's memoirs; two sons—a teenage heroin dealer and a twelve-year-old homosexual; and a dotty mother-in-law who yearns for her pet lizard and her home village. Despite these pressures, both the soapish heroine and her narrative still have time for needy neighbors—a cheerful hooker who longs to go to Las Vegas and a haughty mother who abuses her telekinetic child. Ultimately, downtrodden Gloria kills her troublesome husband, her doper son goes to live with his granny in her home village, and her homosexual prodigal son returns home from the lecherous dentist who "adopted" him just in time to save his despondent mother from suicide.

Matador (1985/86) is an exercise in excess, a stylish psychological thriller with extravagant costumes, lush visuals, and the narrative logic of erotic fantasy. It opens with a montage of violence against women, movie images being watched on a VCR by an ex-matador as he masturbates. Having been gored in the ring, Diego Montes (Nacho Martinez) now only *teaches* bullfighting, but to recapture the ecstasy of the kill, he murders young girls. Angered by the insinuation that he might be a repressed homosexual, Angel (Antonio Banderas), one of Diego's virginal students, tries to rape his next door neighbor Eva, who conveniently (for the Oedipal subtext) just happens to be Diego's young fashion-model mistress. Angel is sexually disturbed, not only by an evil repressive mother who belongs to Opus Dei (an extreme rightwing lay religious organization), but also by a supernatural ability to see the violent and erotic acts of others and to imagine they are his own. Not only does he see the serial murders of his mentor Diego, but also those of his famous female defense lawyer María Cardenal, a beautiful man-killer, with a secret obsession with matadors, which she picked up while watching Diego being gored. Once Diego and María meet in a movie house during the lust-in-the-dust climax of *Duel in the Sun,* these erotic killers see their destiny and give up all other pursuits. Guiding a group of interested parties—Diego's discarded mistress Eva, the maternal psychiatrist (Carmen Maura) who gives Angel loving support, and the police inspector (Eusebio Poncela) who has eyes for Angel and other young men in tight matador pants—Angel and company try to forestall the final fatal orgasm of Diego and María, but they arrive in time only to witness with envy the blissful smiles of the dead lovers.

La Ley del deseo (1986) is another psychological thriller of excess, but this time about two brothers, Pablo and Tina. Pablo (Eusebio Poncela) is a homosexual screenwriter/director who is in love with a young bisexual named Juan (Miguel Molina) and who rewrites Juan's love letters to make them suit his own standard of absolute passion. One of his soft-core films deeply arouses a young spectator named Antonio (Antonio Banderas), who subsequently has his first homosexual experience with Pablo and immediately is transformed into a possessive lover. When Antonio reads the love letter from Juan that was actually written by Pablo, he becomes insanely jealous and murders his rival. Stunned by grief over Juan's murder, Pablo has a car accident and suffers amnesia. Pablo's brother Tina, formerly Tino (brilliantly played by Carmen Maura), is a transsexual actress who loved and was abandoned by her father and who now hates men. The lesbian model she lives with (ironically played by real-life transsexual Bibí Andersen) has deserted both Tina and her own ten-year-old daughter Ada, who now adopts Tina as her mother and falls in love with Pablo. In order to force Pablo to see him after the murder, Antonio seduces Tina and then holds her hostage, so that he will be granted a final hour of love. Although Pablo goes to the assignation with hatred and dread, his feelings are miraculously transformed into love by the purity of Antonio's passion.

Born in 1951 in the small village of Calzada de Calatrava near Ciudad Real, Almodóvar claims he always felt "like an astronaut in the court of King Arthur" and "knew he was born to take on the big cities." By the time he was eight, this quixotic child was living in La Mancha and then in Cáceres, where he studied with the Salesianos and Franciscans and finished his baccalaureate. In 1967, at sixteen, he finally made it to Madrid where he immediately became a hippy and then a white-collar worker at the National Telephone Company. After hours, he became a versatile member of Madrid's artistic underground—doing comic strips for underground magazines; acting in the avant-garde theater group Los Goliardos; recording and performing live in a rock band called Almodóvar y McNamara; publishing journalistic articles, parodic memoirs (under the pen name Patty Diphusa), a porno photo-story, and a novella; and making experimental short films, first in 8mm and then in 16. Even after making his first feature in 1980, he still continued writing and singing. But by the time he made *Entre tinieblas* in 1983, his first film to be sent to a foreign festival and sold outside of Spain, he was launched as an international auteur.

What do you think is the primary appeal of your films, especially of La Ley del deseo *which has had such international success, whereas most Spanish films have had such difficulty in getting international distribution?*
Well, I've been striving for this over the last three years, and I think this is the fruit of my previous work. People know me more now, and it's easier for me to sell a film. On the other hand, I think my films are very contemporary. They represent more than others, I suppose, the new Spain, this kind of new mentality that appears in Spain after Franco dies. Above all, after 1977 till now. Stories about the new Spain have appeared in the mass media of every country. Everybody has heard that now everything is different in Spain, that it has changed a lot, but it is not so easy to find this change in the Spanish cinema. I think in my films they see how Spain has changed, above all,

because now it is possible to do this kind of film here. Not that a film like
The Law of Desire would be impossible to make in places like Germany, London, or the United States.

*Yes, but it would be impossible to have such a film get half of its financing from
the ministry of culture in any of those countries! How would you define "the new
Spanish mentality"?*
I believe that the new Spanish mentality is less dramatic—although I demonstrate the contrary in my films. We have consciously left behind many prejudices, and we have humanized our problems. We have lost the fear of earthly
power (the police) and of celestial power (the church), and we have also lost
our provincial certainty that we are superior to the rest of the world—that
typical Latin prepotency. And we have recuperated the inclination toward
sensuality, something typically Mediterranean. We have become more skeptical, without losing the joy of living. We don't have confidence in the
future, but we are constructing a past for ourselves because we don't like the
one we had.

*Do you think that the appeal of your films also has something to do with their
unique tone? I know that Pauline Kael in her very enthusiastic review of* La Ley del
deseo *stressed the uniqueness of the tone without really describing what it is.*
Well, I would like to think this is one of the reasons because this is the main
difference of my films. Whether they are good or bad, my films are absolutely
different from other Spanish films and even from the other foreign cinema.
I mean you can talk about a lot of influences, everybody has them. But if you
see all of my films, I'm sure you can differentiate them from the others, you
can recognize them. I would like to think this is the main reason for their
international appeal.

How would you define that tone?
It's hard for me to talk about it because I never try to verbalize about my
films, but it's true there is a different tone, even in general. This is something
I'm obsessed with when I'm working with the actors. They have to say my
lines in a different way. Even for me this is something that's very difficult to
explain to them because you have to catch it and you have to feel it. When
I'm shooting, I'm obsessed with creating an atmosphere that explains exactly
what is my tone. The atmosphere that I create when I'm shooting, this is the

tone of my films. To take one example, I used to mix all the genres. You can say my films are melodramas, tragicomedies, comedies or whatever because I used to put everything together and even change genre within the same sequence and very quickly. But the main difference is the private morality. I think one auteur is different from another because he has his own morality. When I say morality, I don't mean ethics, it's just a private point of view. I mean you can see a film by Luis Buñuel and you know exactly that it belongs to Buñuel because it's just the way of thinking.

It seems to me that what lies at the center of your unique tone is what you were describing before, that fluidity with which you move so quickly from one genre to another, or from one feeling or tone to another, so that when a line is delivered, it's very funny and borders on parody and we spectators are just ready to laugh, but at the same time it's erotic and moves us emotionally. In this way, you always demonstrate that you're in control, that you're manipulating the spectator response.
Yes, it takes more care than other styles of acting and shooting. You have to be very careful to control the tone because it can easily run away with you and go too far. Just as you say, in my films everything is just at the border of parody. It's not only parody. It's also the borderline of the ridiculous and of the grotesque. But it's easy to fall over the line.

Other filmmakers who come to mind as doing something similar with tone are David Lynch . . .
Absolutely, I recognize myself a lot in *Blue Velvet*. I love it.

I love that film, too. It allows you to be both terrified and turned on and at the same time it's also hysterically funny. And then there's Fassbinder.
But the difference is that Fassbinder, as a German, doesn't have much of a sense of humor. In *Blue Velvet* you can find a great sense of humor, but *Blue Velvet* is more morbid than my films because there is always an element of naiveté in what I'm doing. It's strangely antithetical because I'm not so naive. But this kind of purity of action, feelings, and spontaneity, that's not in *Blue Velvet*. *Blue Velvet* is darker, sicker, sick in every way. But, with a lot of humor. Do you think there is humor in Fassbinder's films?

Oh yes, although it's always combined with pain.

German culture is so different from Spanish culture. In our culture there is a great sense of humor but not in the German culture. Also, I believe that our culture is more visceral. Intuition and imagination influence us more than reason. There is more adventure and spontaneity. We don't fear disorder or chaos.

Your use of Hollywood melodrama—especially in ¿Qué he hecho? *where two characters go to see* Splendor in the Grass *and in* Matador *where there's a long excerpt from* Duel in the Sun—*it seems similar to the ways in which Fassbinder used Sirk and even Billy Wilder's* Sunset Boulevard *in* Veronika Voss, *where he picked something already very extreme—and then pushed it even further to that borderline of parody. How do you see the relationship between your work and Hollywood melodrama?*

All of the influences on me and all of the film references in my films are very spontaneous and visual. I don't make any tributes. I'm a very naive spectator. I can't learn from the movies that I love. But if I had to choose one master or model, I would choose Billy Wilder. He represents exactly what I want to do.

Which Billy Wilder? His films are so varied!

Both Billy Wilders. The *Sunset Boulevard* Billy Wilder and *The Apartment* Billy Wilder, the *One, Two, Three* and *The Lost Weekend. The Lost Weekend,* for example, is a big, big drama but you can find a lot of humor in it and a lot of imagination in the way it develops a unique situation. It's a great challenge for a screenwriter. But to return to the question about Hollywood, I just love that big period of the classic American melodrama. I'm not just talking about Sirk but about the kinds of films Bette Davis made. I like these extreme genres where you can talk naturally about strong sentiments without a sense of the ridiculous. This is something that melodrama has. But, of course, all these films like *Splendor in the Grass* and *Duel in the Sun,* which is so outrageous, I mean you have to be very very brave to dare to go to this kind of extreme, you can really be grotesque if you don't know how to do it. This is something that I like. But I use the genre in a different way. My films are not so conventional as that kind of melodrama. Because I don't respect the boundaries of the genre, I mix it with other things. So my films appear to be influenced by Hollywood melodrama, but I put in other elements that belong more to my culture. For example, *What Have I Done to Deserve This?* is more like a neorealist film than melodrama. I think it's more like the films of Rossellini, Zavattini, and De Sica—more like Italian neorealism which is also a melodramatic genre. But I put in a lot of humor. That makes the reality even more awful in a way, more extreme. And I also put in a lot of surrealistic elements that completely change the genre. I think that the presence of the nonrational in my films is strong, but I never try to explain it. For example, in *¿Qué he hecho?* I don't try to explain the girl with the telekinetic powers, the girl like Carrie. I just put her in as part of the life or plot, and this kind of element changes the genre.

There's a moment in ¿Qué he hecho? that helps me understand what you might mean by calling it a neorealist film. In one scene the older son asks for help with his homework in assigning the labels "realist" and "romantic" to famous authors, and his granny reverses the traditional answers, calling Byron a realist and Balzac a romantic. Isn't this joke a comment on your own style? Isn't this exactly what you're doing in this movie—reversing the traditional meanings of realist and romantic?
That could be, but I had no consciousness of it.

In one of your interviews, you say you admired very much the Spanish neorealism of Marco Ferreri and Fernando Fernán Gómez, films like El Pisito *(1958),* El Cochecito *(1960) and* La Vida por delante *(1958)—films that combined neorealism with a Spanish absurdist black humor called* esperpento. *In his new book* Out of the Past, *John Hopewell says that ¿Qué he hecho? continues in this tradition.[6] Is this connection valid?*
Yes, very much so. If you have to find some source or relation to Spanish movies for my films, I think they are related to that kind of film. And also to an early film by Francisco Regueiro, *Duerme, duerme, mi amor* (*Sleep, Sleep, My Love*, 1974). It's wonderful. Have you seen that film?

Yes, it's desperately funny, and I can definitely see the connections with the absurdist black humor and the high-rise living theme in ¿Qué he hecho?
Yes, this is one line I admire very much, and also early Berlanga. For me Berlanga's *Plácido* (1961) is a model.

---

[6] John Hopewell, *Out of the Past: Spanish Cinema After Franco*. London: BFI, 1986, p. 239. Although Marco Ferreri is Italian, his earliest features were made in Spain and had enough influence to assure him an important place in the history of Spanish cinema.

Is it the film's rapid pacing and its ensemble of comic characters that appeal to you?
Yes, and also this kind of tragic situation, very dark and very sad, but with great naturalness, and this kind of comedy that talks about a lot of things in life very seriously, and this kind of confusion of a lot of people all talking and doing different things at the same time.

Yes, I can see those qualities in your films, especially in ¿Qué he hecho? . . . I think one of the most amazing things about ¿Qué he hecho? is that whereas it starts out with distanced reflexivity (with Carmen Maura walking past a film crew as she goes to work as a maid in a martial arts gym) and with burlesque (when she mimics their swordmoves with her broom and has a torrid sexual encounter with a man in a shower who proves to be impotent), still amidst all of the satiric absurdities Maura's performance miraculously remains so realistic that she still manages to generate emotional identification in the spectator. And this has a big payoff in the final sequence when she is saved from suicide by the homecoming of her homosexual son who has just walked out on the lecherous dentist his mother left him with in order to cover the dental bill. We still get a big emotional rush from their reunion, and we're marvelling, how did Almodóvar manage to pull this off!
Yes, I tried to do that. This is always the challenge that I face whenever I make a film. . . . I try to solve the problem of how to get the big emotion from the audience, how to get emotional identification with the problem (in this case, high-rise apartment living) which lies behind the facade of absurdity, because everything just under the facade is absolutely real. And I think the audience can always recognize very clearly what I'm trying to say about life in the high-rise. And the jokes have many reasons for being there. For example, the opening titles sequence is very much like an abstract or experimental film with all the crew there making a film while the female protagonist goes to work in that place. That was the square where we were shooting; it was very direct. And in the gym where they're doing kendo, it looks like parody, but it also shows a very aggressive sport—one that releases aggression. And from the beginning you see that she's going to be in a male world and that males are the violent, strong ones who do this kind of thing. And she is just cleaning up. And then she tries to imitate them, just to be more quiet.

It also prepares her for killing her husband with an oxbone.

It's just the surface that's surrealistic, but I think you can understand very well what's just behind that surface. But I always try to work with all of these elements and to make it so that the people can feel it. Another example is the big confession scene in *The Law of Desire* when Carmen Maura, as Tina the transsexual, is trying to tell her brother Pablo about her relationship with their father. You know this is really hard. It's very strange, it's not easy to find a girl like that. Well, but I hope, and I felt that during this speech the audience really identifies with Tina as if she were the girl next door, someone with whom they can readily identify. I mean this is really *heavy*. She committed incest and she changed her sex to be with her father. She's one in a million. In this case, the acting is very important. It's Carmen Maura. If she hadn't been so perfect, then you never could have believed it. To do this kind of thing, you have to be very very careful. But if you succeed with that, then the audience can believe and understand everything.

Even within that scene, you seem to purposely make it even harder for yourself, I mean in the way you set it up with her brother's amnesia, which is a highly contrived and corny way of motivating why Tina has to tell him and the audience about her past at this particular moment. And then that comical touch when she mentions Madrid, and then points out the window, saying, Oh yes, this is Madrid! reminding herself and us of the amnesia. And even with these absurdities, we are still swept away by Maura's performance.

Yes, in that scene even Carmen was very surprised because she told me that when I was directing her, I asked her for exactly the opposite of what she thought was right for this scene. She was sure that everyone else would have asked her to do exactly the contrary of what I said. Because the confession was very quiet, not very dramatic. So perhaps that's why you can believe it better. I don't know.

There seems to be a movement in La Ley del deseo *that is parallel to the one in* ¿Qué he hecho?, *where you start with reflexivity, in this case a film within a film, in which someone dictates from a script how a young man is to masturbate, and a voyeuristic spectator who—*

Imitates what he sees, yes. . . .

In a way, you start out by demystifying how movies work, but then by the end of the film those same dynamics still work on the audience very powerfully. A film-

maker like Buñuel, in showing you how it happens, prevents you from experiencing that kind of pleasure—he offers you a different *kind of pleasure. But you demonstrate how the pleasure works and then make the spectator experience it despite the demonstration.*

Yes, that's true.

My favorite moment in La Ley *is when all the people at the end—Tina, the little girl Ada, and the police—look up with wonder at the window of the apartment where Pablo and his murderous lover Antonio are having their final hour of passionate love.*

Yes, this is one of the moments I'm proudest of—it's like a ritual with the music. I told the cinematographer (Ángel Luis Fernández), make it surprising and magical—not exactly like real magic, but like that moment when everyone looks up at the UFOs in *Close Encounters of the Third Kind.* I like it very much.

It's wonderful. Their faces are full of awe and envy. Even the police are softened and eroticized by the passion they imagine is going on inside that room. They become the quintessential Almodóvar spectators! Isn't this the third time such a spectatorial moment occurs in the film? The first is the opening where Antonio is watching and is turned on by the erotic scene from Pablo's movie. And the second occurs in the middle of the film where Tina asks a man in the street to hose her down while her brother Pablo and the child Ada watch in wonder. Isn't the film's structure controlled by these three spectacular moments?

Yes, all three moments you have mentioned are the key to the film. The beginning is the key to understanding everything. I try to put the spectator into the field that I'm going to explore—the field of desire. Everyone understands that you can pay someone to make love to you. But it's very difficult to recognize that you can pay someone just to *listen* to his desire, which is something very different. This sensual desire is more abstract. It's just the necessity of feeling desire in an absolute way. This is the problem in the film. And also, as you said, I explain how the movie is made. You see just the interior of the movie. But also I explain the director's behavior—the relationship between director and actor. The director, on the one hand, is a voyeur, but he also is pushing, dictating exactly what he wants to be enacted, he wants to be represented, and this is very important to the relationship of power and voyeurism between the director and the actor.

And yet aren't both being controlled by the script, which is probably why the script and the typewriter become so essential in the film—with all those huge close-ups and expressionistic angles of the keyboard? I read in one interview where you say the force of Pablo's imagination is stronger than his feelings and that's why he takes the vengeance on the typewriter—why he refuses to write another script and why he throws the typewriter out the window at the end. But couldn't you also say that the script links Pablo to patriarchal discourse?

I don't understand.

Isn't Pablo like his father—a seducer who prefers young boys and who's never totally committed? Doesn't he reenact his father's seduction of his brother and also inspire his lovers to make a sacrifice? Pablo may want to be in control, but isn't he as shaped by his father as Tina was? Aren't his scripts and movies vehicles for patriarchal ideology?

Well, I didn't think of that. Those are new ideas to me, but I agree with them and find them interesting. I like to discover new explanations in my films. It makes them richer. The opening is the main sequence of desire, of abstract desire rather than of sensual pleasure. Sensuality and physical pleasure are far better represented in the central sequence where Tina says, "Hose me!" than in the opening where the boys says, "Fuck me!" That's an important distinction in the film.

But isn't there submission in both? Aren't they both part of the same masochistic aesthetic that also leads you to put the lust-in-the-dust ending of Duel in the Sun *in the middle of* Matador?

I don't see it as masochism. Masochism requires pain, and I don't find it in my films . . . I don't see masochism even in the Carmen Maura figure Tina, who is so obsessed with her past. She doesn't want to forget anything, even her worst memories. She's very engaged with her worst memories, they even feed her. This can be masochism too . . . a kind of quotidian masochism. In life in general you have to accept pain. It's a kind of adventure and sometimes pain is the price you have to pay; the things you get are more important than the pain. But masochism requires that you *like* to feel pain. . . . No, my films are more about pleasure, sensuality, and living—about the celebration of living. Don't forget you have to be conscious that for this celebration of absolute pleasure, often you have to pay a very high price. But the price is parallel with the pleasure. This is the theory of *Matador*. If you can find an

absolute pleasure, you also have to pay an absolute price. And in the reference to *Duel in the Sun,* there is, of course, what you said, but what was more
important for me in this scene is just that when the ex-matador and lawyer
come to the cinema, they look at the screen and see their future. It's like
when you look into a magic crystal ball. When you go to the cinema, the
cinema reflects not your life but your end. And it was exactly the ending of
Duel in the Sun that is the ending of *Matador.*

But then both in Matador *and* La Ley, *watching movies seems to be a very dangerous activity.*
No, the problem is that *your* mentality is far more rational than ours, than of
the Spanish people. And perhaps all of these terrible things are here inside
my films. But I don't see these elements so clearly. I'm unconscious of them.
I don't want to be so conscious of all these things. You explain everything. I
prefer just to inspire, to suggest, not to explain.

*I'm not really saying there are "terrible things" in your films, I'm just considering
the implications of your choices—like the implications of having your last three
films all end the same way—with an orgasmic climax in which two people are
brought together in a passionate union that is somehow related to suicide and murder. In making this choice, aren't you romanticizing the price one has to pay for
this absolute value? Isn't this a kind of romantic idealism that has connections
with fascism since fascism also glamorizes death and sacrifice in the name of the
ideal?*
That sounds terrible! (laughs) . . . No, the moral of all my films is to get to a
stage of greater freedom. *¿Qué he hecho?* is about the liberation of women,
even if it takes killing. It's very dangerous to see my films with conventional
morality. I have my own morality. And so do my films. If you see *Matador*
through a perspective of traditional morality, it's a dangerous film because
it's just a celebration of killing. *Matador* is like a legend. I don't try to be
realistic, it's very abstract, so you don't feel identification with the things
that are happening, but with the sensibility of this kind of romanticism. I
hope that there is not this kind of fascist element in the celebration of murder. You know, murder happens. I'm not as, what should I say, as "naughty"
as Patricia Highsmith. The kind of murder that horrifies me is the kind that
happens in her novels—among regular people, where you agree with that
murder. This is really immoral.

I think it's your tone that prevents the spectator from taking these murders seriously or from seeing them in terms of traditional morality. I know you've been widely quoted as saying you want to make films as if Franco had never existed, and I think that desire may be related to your refusal to see this potential connection between romantic love and fascism.

Perhaps I didn't fully understand what you said before about my glorification of violence.

It's not just violence, it's violence in the name of a noble sacrifice, which one can also find in Christianity. For example, Tina has an altar in which she puts the image of the Virgin next to that of Marilyn Monroe and Liz Taylor. . . .

The Spanish people are known to be very religious. But it's not true. What we do in general is to adapt religion for our own needs, as Tina does. She needs to lean on something because she feels very much alone. Religion is there to make her feel better, to keep her company. And the altar contains, not only things of beauty, but all of her memories that accompany her, that prevent her from feeling so lonely. This is the kind of religion she needs. For her, there's a virgin and a dictator, and even the toys of the young girl.

Yes, but doesn't the altar serve as the backdrop for the final reunion between Pablo and Antonio, for their passion?

Yes, in the end they form part of the altar, they become religious figures.

That's precisely what I mean. You glorify their kind of romantic love by turning it into a religion, by mystifying it with the same ideological trappings that helped to glorify fascism. But with lots of humor. . . . Maybe it's time to turn to another crucial institution that was glorified by Franco, the family. In one interview you noted that Wim Wenders chose a melodrama about the family (Paris, Texas) *to win the hearts of American spectators.*

That was just a joke. I like using the family very much.

In Spanish films, the family is typically made up of cruel mothers, absent, mythified fathers, and stunted, precocious children. And there seems to be a special Spanish version of the Oedipal narrative with a series of displacements of desire and hostility between the mother and the father. Sometimes the object of desire for the son is transferred from mother to father, as in Le Ley del deseo, *but mostly there's a displacement of the hostility, usually directed at the father, onto the mother. I don't*

find this dynamic in any other national cinema. And this is particularly odd since patriarchal power is so strong, or at least was so strong in Spain under Franco. Is it that the father is so threatening, the son has to displace his hostility onto the mother? Why do you think there's so much hostility directed toward the mother?
I don't know. I defended the mother in *¿Qué he hecho?* Of course, there was also a bad mother next door, but you actually find this kind of mother in Spain—the one who is so repressive to her children.

Yes, but in Matador *the only evil character is not the serial murderers, but Angel's repressive mother from Opus Dei.*
Yes, I find this kind of mother very hateful, but there are several other mothers in that film. . . . I feel very close to the mother. The idea of motherhood is very important in Spain. The father was frequently absent in Spain. It's as if the mother represents the law, the police. It's very curious because in my next film project, I have two young girls kill their mother. When you kill the mother, you kill precisely everything you hate, all of those burdens that hang over you. In this film, I'm killing all of my education and all of the intolerance that is sick in Spain.

Is this matricide an act of liberation or is it suicidal?
I don't want to psychoanalyze it. It's like killing the power. In my film, this is a very typical mother from the South, like Bernarda Alba. In order to frighten her two daughters, she tells them that the world is going to be destroyed and that they will be guilty. And the two girls run away. Then the two parents, both the father and the mother, supposedly die, but the mother doesn't really die. When the two girls become women, the mother suddenly appears like a ghost in order to drive them crazy, really crazy, because she behaves like a ghost. It's very surrealistic. At the end, the two girls have a duel with their mother and then, after they kill her, they discover that she was not a ghost, that she was alive. But she was very crazy. The mother's behavior is actually more murderous than that of the girls.

*It sounds fascinating. I can't think of any other national cinema that has so many matricides as the Spanish cinema. For example, in 1975, the year that Franco died, there were two major films in which matricide occurs—*Furtivos *and* Pascual Duarte. *And later in Saura's* Mamá cumple cien años, *it's attempted again. And*

now your project! And, what's also strange, in Spanish films the killing of the father is only done by daughters, not by sons.
It's true. . . . Fathers are not very present in my films. I don't know why. They are not in my films. This is something I just feel. When I'm writing about relatives, I just put in mothers, but I try not to put in fathers. I avoid it. I don't know why. I guess I'm very Spanish.

I guess you treat fathers like Franco, as if they never existed. . . . What is the name of your new project?
I don't know whether I'm going to change it later, but now it's called *Distant Heels.* I remember when I was a child, it was a symbol of freedom for young girls to wear high heels, to smoke and to wear trousers. And these two girls are wearing heels all the time. After running away, the two sisters live together, and the older remembers that she couldn't sleep until the moment that she heard the sound of distant heels coming from the corridor. I also like the title because it sounds like a Western. All this happens in a desert in the South and the look is like that.

What qualities do you strive for in your mise en scène? *Can you make any generalizations about that? The visual look seems quite different from film to film.*
Yes, they *are* different. I'm learning at the same time that I'm shooting. I didn't go to any film school. So everything I learned, was learned while shooting. Also, I like so many different genres and want to go for very different qualities in each film. I have many different sides and want to develop them all. I'm not obsessed with style. I'd like each film to be absolutely different from the others in every possible way. This is a way of learning everything. And I don't want to get bored.

What impact has your success in Berlin and New York with La Ley *had on your new projects? Has it led to any concrete proposals for the future? Any international coproductions?*
For me the success merely means I can sell my films outside of Spain, and that's good for everybody. Right now I don't feel the temptation to make films outside of Spain because here I can work easier and faster and because it's the culture I know better than any other. I'm sure I'll make a film outside of Spain one day, but not now, not for the moment. Someday I would like to make a film in English, but later. Perhaps I'm lazy. But I want to keep working in this way. I want to feel very independent, and now I have to defend my independence even more than before.

Pedro Almodóvar: Desperado Living

TIM CLARK/1988

PEDRO ALMODÓVAR once wore fishnets and lipstick fronting a
Madrid glam-punk band in the New York Dolls tradition and singing "Yes,
I'm going to be a mama . . . I'm going to have a baby . . . I'm going to call
him Lucifer . . . I dreamed of him living by prostitution . . ." It possibly loses
something in translation from the original Spanish.

This man once published a novel called *Fuego en las entrañas* about a sani-
tary napkin magnate who wreaks revenge on the nine lovers who've jilted
him (ouch!).

This man, under the byline Patty Diphusa, wrote for *La Luna* magazine
the regular confessions of an imaginary international porno star (inspired,
so it is said, by Anita Loos's character, Lorelei Lee, in *Gentlemen Prefer Blondes*,
viz: "Fun is fun but no girl wants to laugh *all* the time").

This man has been compared to John Waters, Buñuel, Fassbinder, even
Billy Wilder. He won a Spanish Ministry of *Culture* award as best new director
for his '87 film *Law Of Desire,* opening here this week, which he also wrote,
about a film director and his brother: the brother had an affair with Daddy
long ago and they ran off to Morocco and the boy had a sex-change to please
Daddy but became a lesbian when Dad ran off with another woman, and
now he-she's back with her brother who's hopelessly in love with a straight
man and her woman has run off leaving her to bring up a daughter, and the
lesbian mum's played by a famous Madrid male transvestite, and the sex-

From *Time Out,* November 1988. Reprinted by permission of Time Out Magazine, Ltd.

change is played by a gloriously self-mocking woman . . . And it's a murder thriller.

You get the picture: we're not talking art movies. And his elastic CV stretches further still. Pedro Almodóvar (stress on the third syllable) fled the life of a horny-handed son of toil in Calzada de Calatrava, his village birthplace in the farmlands of La Mancha, in his teens, to become a hippy in Madrid. He worked on underground magazines and comics in the '60s, performed with the independent theatre company Los Goliardos and as a film extra in the '70s, and supported himself the while as an office worker in the National Telephone company. His early Super-8 efforts at filmmaking, all luridly titled, had him voicing over dialogue and comments during projection, even singing along. A history of "The Avant-Garde Film in Spain" reports they were "crazy parodies of melodramas, love stories, Biblical dramas, retro musicals . . ." exhibiting a "rude and caustic humour, and a mise-en-scène rejoicing in mediocrity, turning stereotypes and clichés upside down."

From here on in, Almodóvar's films are a joyful series of lush ejaculations, his own post-Franco purgative, if you'll excuse the mixed metaphor. His first full-length feature, I blush to report, was called, ahem, *Fuck, Fuck, Fuck Me Tim.* His second—*Pepi, Luci, Bom, and other Girls on the Heap* (1980), a John Waters-ish hommage to punk girls—brought him success at home consolidated by 1982's *Labyrinth of Passions,* a pop movie influenced by Richard "Hard Day's Night" Lester. The soundtrack for *Labyrinth,* composed and performed by Almodóvar, prompted the live concerts and recordings of his group Almodóvar y McNamara.

Dark Habits (*Entre tinieblas,* '83) sees him honing camp Catholic fetishism in a story of a Madrid convent. The Order of Humble Redeemers, which seeks to save hookers, junkies, and murderesses, and resorts to shooting them full of smack to fight declining attendance figures. Mother Superior's a junkie herself, other nuns sing, one of them plays the bongos and fucks her pet tiger. But his movies achieve much more than outrage. The redoubtable Pauline Kael, a movie critic more renowned for autopsies than midwifery, writes of them in such terms as "glamorous, impossibly passionate, hyperbolic romance," "disreputable sensuality" and "bright-colored tragi-comedy." And in Spain he is very much a star. On the streets of Madrid, in the bars, in the clubs, everyone knows him: his audiences at home cross every boundary of class, age, and sex, and he's regularly pestered for autographs by little old ladies.

Near my hotel *La Ultima tentacion de Cristo* is playing on the Gran Via to packed, young houses, apparently without fuss. This, and Almodóvar's success, induces a certain envy, not to say culture shock, since the UK is fast earning itself an unenviable reputation for constipated priggishness and moral censoriousness. Naïvely I ask if the actors who play the gay parts in *Law Of Desire* experience any professional problems, or indeed social ones, given the current Western AIDS phobias.

He is aghast. "You have to accept you're living in a country under heavy censorship, and I feel very sorry for you. England twenty years ago was the inspiration for us, we imitated you, you were an icon. Now it is our turn. The last time I was there, eighteen months ago, everything had changed. The only thing you have going for you now is hairdos. And the kind of sexual intolerance you mention is more dangerous than AIDS itself. No, the actors have had no problem with their careers or lives, just the opposite, they were very successful with these roles. I have to say that none of the actors were gay. That's easier for me as director because then they act, they *represent,* they are not reliving. I prefer absolutely to have Carmen Maura, a real woman, represent a transsexual. Though I was more nervous filming the sex bits than the actors were." But Almodóvar achieves the equivalent of getting a Spanish Matt Dillon to wear his knees behind his ears, effortlessly. "I wanted it to look fresh and natural and these straight people proved so natural about their bodies, they had no shame about their physicality, no sense of something unnatural or prohibited. And after the first half an hour, the audience forget that the lovers are men; they accept it as a love story. That's a big change in Spain and really healthy.

"Passion is the real protagonist in this film. Everyone can identify with how it develops through the three characters: movie-maker, his lover, his sister. There's lots of promiscuity and I know it's courageous to do it now but I'm talking about the opposite of AIDS, the sensuality of bodies and a celebration of that is important."

Like Buñuel, he seems to work with a core of regular faces, but playing drastically different roles in each film.

"In all the films there's always someone new. But I do like having an artistic family, like a stable repertory, which is sincere and concrete, though I don't trust in the conventional family at all.

"I work very hard on how the actors express the dialogue, how they *walk* and *talk*. And when they pick up an object I want it to be very physical—not obvious, but definite. For instance the hose sequence [where Carmen Maura, hot, bothered, and frustrated in the night shouts at a street-cleaner to drench her] is *very* physical; I made her a giant on the screen. It's a great release. It's something I've always dreamed of doing." Me as well, I interrupt. "Everybody says that but you are too shy. I always loved it in *La dolce vita* where Anita Ekberg walks into the fountain, the Fontana de Trevi.

"Madrid becomes a person in my films. The stories are invented through my life. Details are important, I know the quotidian details of this town; it is my language. In America [where his movies are big in all the cities where the trash aesthetic and Spanish tongue are widespread] they asked me to work, but I'm afraid of the change of culture. We were growing together, Madrid and me, over the last twelve years. I feel very close to this town. I go to the market, I live like a housewife. I make everything myself, and I want to know everything that happens in the street outside at every different hour."

Does he still dabble in the other arts? "I feel absorbed by film at the moment. The band was very funny, it was school-of-ironic-punk, and people of my generation all dream of being on stage, but the press and everybody took it too seriously. But at that time I needed that direct contact with the audience. Right now it's not for me, but I still write every day."

Much later, taking my leave of Madrid, and the night air, from the terrace viewpoint over western Madrid in the Jardines de Ferraz, a woman cruises slowly by me, her long skirt flicking about her legs. She stands studying me a little way off, and melts into the darkness of the bushes. But wait! She was over six foot and had *very* large hands. Aah, Madrid! No wonder *our* Queen's visit went down like a lead balloon.

Pedro Almodóvar on the Verge . . .
Man of La Mania

VITO RUSSO/1988

PEDRO ALMODÓVAR can't figure out why the Parker Meridien Hotel on 56th Street has a sign in the lobby saying "Non-Smoking Rooms Available."

"Why does anyone need a non-smoking room?" he asks. "It's *your* room. If you don't smoke then don't smoke in your room!" He throws his hands up in confusion. "Anyway, it seems Americans are crazy about this issue right now. In Europe we have *mandatory* smoking." We both light cigarettes.

This is our third annual interview. The first was after he made *What Have I Done to Deserve This?* in 1986, the second a year ago after *Law of Desire* opened, and now because his latest film *Women on the Verge of a Nervous Breakdown* opened the 26th New York Film Festival. In the last three years Almodóvar has emerged as the singular voice of Spanish cinema, the personification and spiritual father of "La Movida," the all-purpose phrase coined in Madrid to signify life after Franco, sexual freedom, punk rockers, sunshine, great food, good times, and the general explosion of creative expression that a nation experiences when moving from a dark past of repression into the light of freedom.

Each of Almodóvar's films has created an alternative world based in political reality but transformed by crackpot, sometimes surreal, fantasies of the way life should be in an amoral society. His characters, from the glue-sniffing housewife in *What Have I Done* to the transsexual heroine of *Law of Desire*, owe their salvation to an absolute commitment to personal freedom regard-

From *Film Comment*, November/December 1988.

less of the consequences. In *What Have I Done* the housewife has a dreary life so she sells her youngest son to a gay dentist, murders her husband with a ham bone, and cooks the weapon for dinner. In the end, she's happy. In *Law of Desire* and *Matador,* sexual and emotional passion are everything. In both films, dead bodies litter the screen at fade out time, but they die *happy,* for ecstasy.

"This is the most important thing," says Almodóvar as we settle down to talk. "It is *crucial.* This is what life is about—to be completely unrepentant—otherwise what did your life mean? What was it about?"

Nowhere is this philosophy more dramatically rendered than in *Matador,* in which a bullfighter who gets off on violence meets his match in a female lawyer obsessed with sex and death. The merger becomes the perfect love affair. When they are found dead by the police, an officer says, "I've never seen such happiness." It is Almodóvar's only flop in Spain, where casting aspersions on bullfighting is like spitting on God.

His career reads like a simple case of overnight sensationalism. He's a child of the fifties who fled the small village of Calzada de Calatrava to become a telephone operator in Madrid. When a reporter recently asked one of his idols, Lily Tomlin, when she decided to leave her hometown of Detroit, she replied, "As soon as I realized where I was." Almodóvar howls at this: In La Mancha he felt "like an astronaut at King Arthur's court." So at sixteen (like Tomlin's Ernestine) he went to work for the telephone company in Madrid, moving from telephone operator to pop star to household word in a hot decade. Now he makes a film a year.

"I hope I can keep up the rhythm," he says, settling onto a sofa with a touch of exhaustion. "This is all very nice and exciting, but it's difficult for me to write and to work, because I'm traveling all the time. I need very much to go back to work now. The more success you achieve, the less time you have, and that is a pity." He smiles broadly. "I absolutely promise you to make a film every year."

The film that has brought him to the festival this year is his most colorful, most accessible, and funniest film to date. It's exclusively about women and their willingness to express dangerous emotion, illustrating his firm conviction that "men cry, but I think women cry better." On the face of it, *Women on the Verge* is about an actress whose boyfriend has taken a powder. She keeps *meaning* to jump out the window or take sleeping pills, but her spirit is so strong that she and everyone else in the film end up swooping around on broomsticks to the delightful tunes of La Lupe.

It's a movie about earrings and burning beds and people who throw the telephone out the window when their lovers leave. It's based on Jean Cocteau's *The Human Voice* the way "Mack the Knife" is about Hitler. In fact it owes more to Jean Louis than Jean Cocteau. It's a film that probably couldn't have been made by a director who happens to be heterosexual. The opening credits bring back *Funny Face*. The decor and fashions echo Frank Tashlin. The performances recall *Twentieth Century*. It stars the by-now-familiar Almodóvar stock company, including the superbly gifted Carmen Maura. It's a terrific hit in Spain; the word "Almodóvarian" has come to mean "when things get just a little bit too crazy."

Almodóvar has a joyous stance toward his films. He's Woody Allen without the angst and Martin Scorsese without guilt. From the beginning he has said repeatedly that his work and his films are meant to "deny even the *memory* of Franco" by creating a world in which the disenfranchised are able to be the masters and (especially) mistresses of their own destiny. Any discussion of *Women on the Verge of a Nervous Breakdown* necessarily begins with the way the film looks, a result of Almodóvar's cinematic education.

"The aesthetics of the film are purely Frank Tashlin," he says, "but at the same time it's my vision of what I loved about those films twenty years later."

So it's not a copy, and it's not an homage. It's more that in a very real sense he's incorporated into his work what the movies of his adolescence looked like.

"The films I saw have a huge and deep relationship with me and with my education. I had a very dark and awful education by priests. But at the same time I went to the cinema and the movies starring Natalie Wood and Elizabeth Taylor. But especially the films made from Tennessee Williams were my second education—which was stronger and more powerful than the priests'. You know, at that moment, watching those films, I *felt* like a sinner. I was twelve or thirteen, and *Cat on a Hot Tin Roof* absolutely corrupted me. I felt at that moment . . . I recognized that I belonged to the world of this film in which there were sinners and not to the world of the priests. So the movies were a kind of intimate and private education for me.

"I remember Frank Tashlin movies with a certain kind of housewife, who I didn't know if she actually existed, but was a kind of artificial and false image that has a powerful truth for me, which I can't explain. I look at it with humor, but it very much belongs to my sensibility. They don't belong to my fantasies, those movies, they belong very much to my reality."

The trashy movies of the fifties condemned by the Catholic church were actually blatant lessons in the prevailing morality. The world of the fifties for a Catholic in any country included scanning the "condemned" list and listening to that flaming queen Cardinal Spellman ban *Baby Doll* from the pulpit of St. Patrick's cathedral without even having seen it—much like the zealots stationed outside the Ziegfeld more than twenty-five years later carrying on about *The Last Temptation of Christ.* It was the era of the "bad girl" movie starring Cleo Moore and Beverly Michaels, melodramas that took a page from Cecil B. De Mille and that graphically spelled out the excesses they condemned.

These were the films of Almodóvar's youth. "Inevitably you fashion your own world from the past," he says. "I like big melodramas, but I can't actually make a big melodrama because my point of view is amoral. I can't take those stories and believe the underlying morality, which is the basis for melodrama. I have different morals from that period. Bad-girl movies are very moral. They invest themselves in a collective belief that there is good and bad behavior. This is a rule of the genre. So I cannot really make those films again. I can respect the rules of the genre, which I love, but my sensibility is something which I think belongs to the eighties. You can't be so innocent. You can't be so naive any longer, even if you like that genre.

"In my films bad girls are not bad. They have the classic look so you can enjoy it, but there is no judgment. I love Douglas Sirk, but I can't make a Sirk film because I'm not so upset over those old issues of morality. I just use them. Latin people know that there is a period of the early sixties in American movies that belongs completely to America, and they can see it in *Women on the Verge.* Many American comedies were inspired by French authors, a sensibility also present in my film. *Women* looks like a farce, like *Cactus Flower,* but it's about female loneliness in a penthouse. These women are abandoned, alone, sad; they are very fragile, and you have to see this, too, in a very serious way.

Publicist Marcie Bloom is figuratively and good-naturedly tapping her foot in the next room because this is film festival week and at any given moment it's always time for the director of the minute to move on to the next critic of the eternal. Since, after twenty-five years, the New York Film Festival has still not seen fit to create a hospitality suite, we do the next best thing. We decide that what we really need to do is go out and continue this discussion over a terrific drag act—John Epperson as Lypsinka, mistress of the *film-fatale* send-up. The following Saturday night Almodóvar, four critics, two publicists, and a distributor preconvene at my house. Everyone is watching a video of *The Day the World Ended*. Adele Jergens plays the last striptease artist left on Earth after a nuclear war. Almodóvar beckons me into my office and presents me with the screenplay for his next film and a snapshot of his boyfriend in Madrid. "I wanted you to have something that is very me. These are the two obsessions in my life at this moment."

We've got an hour before Epperson's *I Could Go on Lip-Synching* starts at midnight. Since we're all in a fun mood, I broach the subject of how rude *Women on the Verge* isn't compared to his previous work. The crowd in the living room is gaga over a tape of Bette Midler on the United Jewish Appeal telethon.

"It's not rude at all," he says. "But I'm very glad of that because after *Law of Desire* I wanted to make something more optimistic and fun because I needed it. I make movies for my needs. My goal has never, never, never been to make shocking movies.

"*Women on the Verge* is like a daughter of *Law of Desire* because it's inspired by *The Human Voice,* which I used in that film. I was very excited and impressed by Carmen's scene in *Law of Desire,* and I wanted to continue this play in a different context, in a progression. Carmen, in both films, is a very painful figure. In *Desire* she is an abandoned son who becomes a woman, and in *Women* she is also abandoned, but she doesn't suffer so much. She finds a lot of strength. She mixes a gazpacho with sleeping pills but forgets to drink it. There is hope here."

One of the funniest bits in *Women* is an old white-haired lady reading the news on TV. Turns out she's Pedro's mother. "I brought her from the country to do this one scene," he laughs. "This belongs to my theory of the movie that everything is the way we want it to be—in my film an old lady can be a newscaster. Which of course will never happen in real life."

Speaking of real life, I mention that I recently saw a print of *Valley of the Dolls* in a gay bar on Fire Island. What was so funny about it was how serious it was originally meant to be. "Yes, of course," says Almodóvar. "That was the kind of innocence I was talking about before. We can't do exactly that ever again, but we are the perfect audience for that film, and it gets better with time. Gay men understand certain things about emotions, which are usually designated as feminine. The stereotype is that gay men are, therefore, 'like' women. This, of course, is rubbish. We keep on being what they call masculine in behavior while staying in touch with a different side of human emotions."

Almodóvar's cultural background and education dictate, however, that there are certain things labeled masculine that will not be disposed of so easily. The opening scene of *Law of Desire* is a case in point. It shows a man being directed in an erotic film sequence to say to another man, "Fuck me, fuck me." For Almodóvar, this was nearly impossible to get through.

"I don't know if I told you," he says quite seriously, "but I was really uneasy during the shooting of that scene—me, Pedro Almodóvar, personally. Much more uneasy than the actors. I even told them that I could never do that scene if I were an actor. The actors weren't gay in that scene, and I think it's easier if you're not gay. It is very difficult for men, straight or gay, to overcome our education. The scene is almost like a horror movie for some people in the degree of discomfort it causes audiences. They wanted me to cut it in England. Originally, all I wanted was one naked body in front of the camera and the voice of the director telling him what to do, but I just couldn't bear it; it was too intense, and in the end I added cutaway shots to the director and his assistant just to relieve some of the tension. I couldn't even say the words 'fuck me' in direction. This machismo education is never going to go away. And I'll tell you something, I'm afraid of knowing that. I'm afraid of being conscious of that. It frightens me to know that I will never get rid of that education. I don't like to think about the truth of that."

At the New Director's screening of *Law of Desire* at the Museum of Modern Art, the film was immediately criticized by a well-known cinematographer as shocking for "promoting homosexuality in this day and age," an obvious reference to the AIDS crisis.

"What can I say about this problem?" he sighs wearily. "One must continue to explore romanticism and sexuality on the screen. There is a kind of awful conservative morality that has developed since AIDS which is frightening and dangerous. Like when the Pope—who is *really* crazy—tells people that AIDS is a judgment of God. I think we have to be very radical right now on these issues. It seems to me that all the freedoms we have won can disappear very quickly. I feel I have a personal duty right now to be very radical in defending individuality above all.

"*Law of Desire* is a film about a man so obsessed with possessing the soul of someone he loves that he is willing to lose his life in exchange for one hour alone with him. This isn't a tragedy. It would have been a tragedy if he couldn't have had that one hour. I never make obvious political statements in my films, but I think it is very clear what I think about the world in which I live. And aside from *The Battle of Algiers,* there aren't very many good overtly political films. But when I talk about the crazy life of a housewife in *What Have I Done* it's political, and I prefer to do it like that.

"*What Have I Done* is absolutely a Socialist film. This is something a Communist has to do . . . to tell a story like that today in Spain. The films of [Pier Paolo] Pasolini were exceptionally political in that way. All of his ideas about class and society are in his films. Look at *Mamma Roma.* My films are political in the sense that I always defend the autonomy and absolute freedom of the individual—which is very dangerous to some people."

It's almost midnight, and everybody moves to the Provincetown Playhouse in the Village where more critics from the festival are piling into their seats to see Epperson conjure Lypsinka, who recreates the fun-house mirror essence of some obscure performers of the forties and fifties and what they meant to us. We're not talking Judy Garland and Marilyn Monroe here. This is Nanette Fabray singing "Louisiana Hayride."

Almodóvar loves it. "It is so *cinematic,*" he tells Epperson backstage. "Come to Spain, and I will find the theater. The language of this show is universal because everyone knows Connie Francis and Vikki Carr."

"Everything has changed in this decade," says Almodóvar. "Everything. You can't trust any ideology in the same way that you did once. After the militancy of the sixties, the superficiality of the eighties generation is actually a very active political gesture. You have to be conscious of it."

We pass an ad for *Matador,* and it says simply, "A New Film by Almodóvar." I ask how it feels to have only one name like Hitchcock and Garbo.

"You were right from the very beginning," he chuckles wickedly. "You discovered me, and you were absolutely right! But I don't feel it or think about it. My problems are the same: always the next script, always the difficulties in writing it. I think it's more spectacular if you look at me from the outside and see only 'Almodóvar' in print. Now the Spanish press says, 'This is an Almodóvarian situation' or 'an Almodóvarian person,' but I don't like it. When they say that, I feel misunderstood.

"What's wonderful is to notice that people want to see my movies. And that by the miracle of communication I am able to put my obsessions, my problems, my life on the screen and have them reach an audience. That impresses me tremendously. But curiously it doesn't make me feel more sure of myself as an artist. Each time I start a new movie I know that I want to make that movie, but I don't know if I will know *how* to do it.

"I feel very sad that I'm becoming like a moral example. I was the guy working very hard at the telephone company, struggling to make my movies, and now in the same town I have two films playing. It's like a melodrama. I find it funny, but at the same time there's something sad about it.

"I want to think that I am now constructing my next past—you understand? When I was a child, my past was what I saw on the screen, and now I'm constructing what will represent my next past in my own movies. The difference between the dark past and now is that I am able to create a future of my own construction on film. It's a future that I decide to have."

Pedro has to go back to Spain. He is returning to New York for the opening of *Women on the Verge* and has a dinner date then with Lily Tomlin with whom he'd love to work. "A few years ago I might have jumped at the chance to work here because I wasn't sure of what I wanted. Now I think success has come to me when I am mature enough to know better what I want. I'm glad to make what I want to make in my own country. If I ever come here to make movies, the time will be right or not at all."

As he gets into the car we finish up the last important piece of business. In *Women on the Verge* Carmen Maura wears a spectacular pair of earrings—two espresso coffeepots dangling halfway to her shoulders. Everyone in New York wants to know where he found them. "I had them made for the film. If I can find them, I'll send them to you."

Interview with Pedro Almodóvar

PHILIPPE ROUYER AND CLAUDINE
VIÉ / 1988

Q : *Can you tell us about your life before you started making films?*
A : First of all, I lived. I was born in La Mancha and I left for Madrid just
about twenty years ago. I came to the capital city to make a life for myself.
That was the most important thing. So I started to write, to do theater, underground cinema and many other things. My first commercial film came out
in 1980.

Q : *What relationship do you still maintain with the "Movida" of Madrid?*
A : I have a hard time discussing this because people only talk about "Movida" outside of Spain. In Spain, you never talk about it. We are all very independent artists, and we don't cultivate a relationship among ourselves. I
continue to make films and the others continue to do what they do. Those
who are talented develop, those who aren't just keep on going. We don't
really discuss the question.

Q : *Under what conditions did you make your first Super-8 films?*
A : Already as a kid I used to write stories. Starting in 1970 I began telling
stories through images. I did it always with friends and on location so we
wouldn't need lights. I tackled all the different genres, including those super-
productions *à la* Cecil B. De Mille, with lots of costumes and props. It was
like a game, but from the very beginning it was tied to a visceral need to tell

From *Positif,* vol. 327 (1988). Translated from French by Paula Willoquet-Maricondi.
Reprinted by permission.

stories through images. Even though we were not doing tracking shots, shooting in Super-8 offered us just about all the range of cinematic expression. At that time, I was financing my own films because they were inexpensive; everyone gave what they could.

Q : *How did you start making commercial films?*
A : It was a logical progression. My first film, *Pepi, Luci, Bom, and Other Girls on the Heap,* was made in the same way I made my Super-8 films. Except that many of my friends thought I should use a different format. So we shot it on 16 mm, without any money, on weekends. Whenever we had a little money, we would buy film and shoot a few scenes. We did this for a year and a half. It wasn't easy, but we learned a lot. Everyday, we had to change the script, rewrite some scenes. I was haunted by the word "end." It took me a year and a half, but I made it.

Q : *How was this first film received?*
A : It was a surprise. It was both a scandal and a great success. It was a very Spanish film, but nobody had ever made a film quite like this one. It carried a great deal of joy, the absence of any memory of Franco. In my films, not only are Spain's past and the civil war absent, but they are consciously rejected. For many, it was a revolution. In any event, *Pepi, Luci . . .* enabled me to make a second film.

Q : *We did not see your first film in France, but we were being told that it carried certain pornographic traits.*
A : I don't really know how to define pornography. I don't think there was any in my film. There were some "strong" scenes but shot with a lot of spontaneity, which made them "acceptable." Pornography for me has to do with intentions. I think we can do anything; it all depends on the intention, the characters, the situations.

Q : *From your very first films, you have always privileged humor. Is this in your nature or do you use humor so you can get away with commenting on Spanish society?*
A : It's in my nature, but it's also a narrative element, like a kind of lubricant I use so my stories can be more easily assimilated. If you took out the humor in *Law of Desire,* it would become an unbearable story. Sometimes the humor

is ambiguous, but I think it's an element that is always present in my life. Even dramatic events have their humorous side.

Q: *What is your view of Spanish cinema?*

A: Spanish society has changed a lot, but its cinema hasn't. These changes have taken place in particular areas, like fashion, design, music . . . in those areas that afford more independence and demand less money. In cinema, the stories are still very similar to the ones we used to tell, but with a few changes. Every year there are some films that catch my attention. In many cases, they are made by people who end up not being commercially successful. I really like *El Desencanto [The Disenchantment]* by Jaime Chávarri. Also, Berlanga's first films were, to my mind, absolute works of art. More recently, I've enjoyed the films of Bigas Luna and those of Victor Erice. But these are very particular films, made by independent filmmakers, very personal.

Q: *Already with your second film,* Labyrinth of Passions, *you are beginning to develop your thematic universe. You seem to be making fun of the sexual adventures of your contemporaries and all your characters are interconnected in complex ways. Why?*

A: I think *Labyrinth of Passions* evokes well the mood in Madrid in the early '80s, the period that became known as the "Movida." I wanted to make a comedy that was very pop, along the lines of Richard Lester in the '70s, but less caustic than *Pepi, Luci . . .* that referenced more Russ Meyer, John Waters, or Andy Warhol. *Labyrinth of Passions* is softer; I made fun of style. Madrid was the most modern center in the world. If you wanted to, you could find the Shah's son, Dalí, and the Pope. I conceived the film along the lines of Billy Wilder's comedies. It's not an easy one, but I love the genre.

Q: *How did you come up with the idea for the setting of your third film,* Dark Habits, *that is, inside a convent?*

A: Like most people of my generation, I received a religious upbringing. However, I don't want to make a film about priests, because I don't like to talk about myself in the first person; I like to hide behind characters and situations. I wanted to make a kind of typical melodrama, like the films of Marlene Dietrich, of Sara Montiel, where the same woman would have a million different adventures: join a convent, become a singer . . . And, at the same time, I wanted something different. I wanted to evoke a feminine universe, totally defined and limited by the parameters of the convent but where, paradoxically, the women become free and autonomous beings, where the reason for their lives there (that is, God and the religious order) takes on secondary importance. In addition to all of that, I wanted to tell a great love story, a story of irrational love in which the heroine would constantly do extraordinary things.

Q: *What was the meaning of the tiger?*
A: For many people, the tiger stands in for the male principle. For me, it was more the presence of the irrational, which is just as natural and believable. And then, there are things that can't be explained, or rather, that I don't like to have to explain because they are not supposed to be explained. From that standpoint, my films have something in common with those of Buñuel. The irrational has to be presented just like it is, without explanations, but treated in a very naturalistic way.

Q: *Have you been pursuing your other artistic interests?*
A: No. I had to quit singing and doing theater. The cinema is like a vampire lover; it doesn't let you do other things. The further I go, the more time I have to devote to the making of a film. I barely have the time to write stories and magazine articles. Before, I was less conscious. I was having fun playing with all these artistic activities. To tell you the truth, I stopped singing when it was no longer fun.

Q: *Can you tell us about your rock group, Almodóvar y McNamara?*
A: Everything was spontaneous. We needed two songs for *Labyrinth of Passions*. I wrote them with a few of my friends. The film was well received and so were the songs, so we recorded an album. We were giving public performances and people were asking us for new songs. The whole thing was pretty funny and on top of that our songs were parodies. We were parodying pop, funk, rock, with very crude language and we were very critical toward our surroundings. Visually, we were a mix between Prince and the Sex Pistols.

Q: What Have I Done to Deserve This?, *like* Law of Desire *later, is the story of a family. Is this just a narrative element or are you defending certain values?*
A: For me, the family is a dramatic subject of great importance. It can be the basis to a great many films.

At first, the family was for me a very oppressive element which society used to limit the freedom of its youth. In spite of that, I had to acknowledge the role that the family plays in the life of a human being. It's a blood tie, almost animal-like and, in any event, irreplaceable. I speak about the dissolution of the family in my films, but I also talk about all that is authentic in familial relationships. For that matter, I should talk about my own origins, my parents' socioeconomic milieu, and about the mother figure . . .

What Have I Done . . . was my first great success; I started being taken seriously after this film. Before that, I had the reputation of being too modern. When the film came out, people were saying: "he is modern, but he has a heart." This film refers back to a genre of which I'm particularly fond: neo-realist films. But it's a neo-realism for today, less melodramatic, but more biting than the Italian neo-realism. However, while making the film, I did think about Rossellini's and De Sica's films, which are, in fact, very close to our own culture.

Q : *In* What Have I Done . . . *you mix artistic worlds and cultures: Operetta, Hollywood, Nazi Germany. What are you after with this patchwork?*

A : This eclecticism somewhat corresponds to my way of life, to my undisciplined personality. I am incapable of taking on one genre and of respecting all its rules. Spontaneously, I mix all the genres in one film, like in the dining room of *What Have I Done* . . . This is in part due to the fact that I approach all stories as if they were cartoons where you're more concerned with immediate events rather than with explaining character behavior. Although my characters have a psychological foundation, I am more interested in watching them live, in watching them get entangled. Life is full of surprises. All day long, we face situations that relate to very different genres. The mere closing of a door can prompt me to switch genres. It's my way of being and of telling stories.

Q : *The little girl who is telekinetic foreshadows the main character in* Matador. *Why these leaps into the fantastic?*

A : The character in *Matador* (Angel), like the little girl in *What Have I Done* . . . , are unhappy and abused. But they're also alike because they both represent two surrealist elements in the films. What I was trying to say with the little girl is that a person who starts life in a hostile environment will develop extraordinary capacities to struggle against this environment, if they are intelligent. Angel's situation is more unclear, more dramatic. His mother told him so many times that he was an idiot, that everything was his fault,

and she so often treated him like an assassin that he developed an unbeliev-
able guilt feeling. Once he figures out that this feeling does not correspond
to any reality, he starts acting like an assassin in order to feel more at peace.
Like his mother, one of those Opus Dei fanatics who still exist in Spain and
who is full of obsessive ideas, he develops a particular sensitivity to death
and all that is monstrous. It's a surrealist element and, psychologically, it's
also a metaphor for a certain kind of Spanish upbringing, one that completely warps young people's minds.

Q : *You hardly move the camera in* What Have I Done . . . *and you also show a
preference for unusual angles. Why?*
A : For many reasons. First of all, the film was shot almost entirely in studio
but they blew it with the house. I could not move the camera and had to use
the tripod all the time. Paradoxically, the tripod was perfect for the film; it
added a great deal of tension. Generally, tracking shots tend to soften the
action while the tripod hardens it. In this case, I could not move the camera
but I also did not want to move it. On the other hand, I wanted to stay inside
the house because it was Gloria's only universe. Except for the lizard, the
only witnesses to her murder are not beings but her refrigerator and gas
stove. I framed the shots from within these domestic appliances because I
wanted to tell the story from the perspective of the objects that were a part
of her daily life. At the same time, I wanted to show the flip side of all these
ads that always tout the happiness brought by domestic appliances but never
the misery that envelops the housekeeper, the lack of pleasure that these
appliances bring.

Q : *In the attempted suicide scene, on the other hand, you use almost a long tracking shot.*
A : That was a difficult scene to shoot because of the lack of space. I started
with a shot of Gloria and then moved to a complicated tracking shot, with
the camera surveying her entire field of vision before returning to her. I really
wanted to use an original shot. The effect is pretty deep, it renders what is
most intimate in a human being. I wanted to show that the moment she
becomes free, free from any obligation, she comes back home and finds it so
neat and ordered that she feels terrible, because there's nothing for her to
do. Her life has no meaning. She worked for her family her entire life, never
taking time to do something for herself, to have hopes. She feels the empti-

ness created by everybody's departure, a huge abyss opens under her. But she is saved by her youngest son's arrival.

Q: *For each new film since* What Have I Done . . . *you use the same technical crew: Ángel Luis Fernández (cinematographer), José Salcedo (editor), Bernado Bonezzi (composer). Are they a team, friends, part of the Almodóvar family?*
A: A little of each. We are more like a theatrical troupe with a core group. I work with them because I like them, and when you have spent so much time together it's easier to work together. We understand one another well; there is great complicity.

Q: *Does the same apply to the talent: Carmen Maura, Eusebia Poncela, Antonio Banderas?*
A: My relationship with the actors is more neurotic.

Q: *What can you tell us about your cinematographer?*
A: Ángel is not a typical cinematographer; he does not fit into any category. I like his extraordinary intuition. His knowledge of lighting is closely tied to his life, to nature. He is an adventurer; when he finishes a film, he takes off alone, goes I don't know where to experience all sorts of dangerous and extraordinary things. I get along well with him, but in a very particular way. When I show him photographs or paintings that I would like to use as references, he seems to know intuitively things that don't depend on words nor on the images I showed him. I appreciate his collaboration.

Q: *Are you involved with the editing of your films?*
A: Yes, of course. It's a big game for me. In the whole process of putting together a film, the editing is my favorite part.

Q: *How's your writing going? Do you work on several scripts at the same time?*
A: I'm always writing several things at the same time. It comes to a point, though, when I have to focus on a single story. Writing is a nightmare for me. Often, when I'm in bed, I have to get up to write because I have all these ideas and images bouncing around in my head. I file them away so I can use them later, but it's like a bad dream that keeps me from getting rest. It's a way of reacting to what I experience during the day. Yesterday, for example, I read a ridiculous review of *Law of Desire,* published in *Cahiers du cinéma.*

They kept talking about the "oral" nature of the film, in relation to *La Voix humaine* . . . Totally idiotic . . . I had talked all day long and at night, when I went to bed, I had the idea of making a film about a mute filmmaker. That way I would not have to give interviews and the film would have a shot at pleasing the *Cahiers* critics. Initially, it was just a joke; but I have started writing it and as soon as I get back to Madrid I'm going to get to work on this story of a filmmaker who becomes mute while shooting a film. The crew takes advantage of the situation to do as they please and the incident brings about a true revolution on the set. Which just goes to show you that it might be better sometimes if the director keeps his mouth shut and goes away (laughter).

That's where I am right now, but seriously, someday I'll make a film about a character who uses language in his profession and who has to find another way of communicating when he can no longer speak. For example, he'll start working with mute people. I started to work on that idea last night: I was learning to use sign language and I was imagining a musical comedy played by deaf mutes (by means of play-back). And all that thanks to *Cahiers du cinéma*.

Q : *Your last two films seem to be built on the same foundation.*
A : That's correct. They are two sides of the same coin.

Q : *Do you think death is the only outcome of passion?*
A : I'm afraid so. I was not able to control the ending of the last two stories. When I sit down to write, I always think I have all the freedom in the world. However, in both cases, I had wanted to end up somewhere different. The ending was imposed on me by the rigor of the stories. These two stories, deep down, are about the same thing: one is about sexual pleasure and the other one is about desire. Well, desire can only be satisfied through sexual pleasure. *Matador* is a very abstract film in a way, like a fable or a legend, although it's very concrete as well. *Law of Desire* is a very concrete film that deals with an abstraction. *Matador* is unreal while *Law* . . . evokes that absolute desire for passion in a life that is very routine.

Q : *Up to* What Have I Done . . . *women have been the driving force of your films.*
A : But even in my last film, the one I shot after *Law of Desire*.

Q: *Are you a feminist?*

A: *Matador* and *Law of Desire* were challenges. I wanted to know how I would get along in a masculine universe. But the feminine world is more fascinating to me. Women are more interesting, richer, more varied, more surprising. Men are all one thing.

Q: *In* Matador, *like in your other films, you make a brief appearance.*

A: It's fun and it flatters my narcissistic side; but, in the end, I only resort to this when I'm missing a character.

Q: Matador *and* Law of Desire *both begin with a masturbation scene. Are you trying to be provocative? In any case, sex is very important in your films.*

A: Fundamentally, it's a narrative strategy. In an opening sequence, you have to try to give as much information as possible about the main character.

In *Matador,* Diego is masturbating in front of the television in which you can see a parade of images of women who have been killed. That way, I'm already linking him to death; let's not forget that in real life he teaches his pupils the art of killing. In this sequence, I'm also explaining that what turns him on the most sexually is the woman about to die from a violent death. This preference will be reinforced later in the film.

In the opening sequence of *Law of Desire,* I let you know the main character's profession and show you the relationship between an actor and his director. The actor is always naked in front of the camera—and sometimes it's quite dramatic, believe me. The actor is helpless in relation to the filmmaker who can read him. In front of this demi-god, the actor is transparent. That's what makes the actor fragile and the filmmaker's power terrifying. He tells him what he wants, and the actor does it, precisely, as if he were an animal. This first scene is neither erotic nor pornographic; it's pathetic. Anyone can understand that a boy might get paid to have sex. What is worse is that someone is paying so he can hear that he is wanted. It's very different and much stronger. There is a kind of absolute dissatisfaction at the level of desire for this filmmaker, it's something he will never have. And that's what he is paying for.

Q: *What is the role of religion and of the "little miracles" in all your films?*

A: For me, they belong to Spanish culture and are a kitsch element (laughter). It's as fascinating as the world of soap operas; it interests me tremendously. The miracle is also a surrealist and absurd element. I don't believe in miracles, but I think it's funny that there are people who do. In fact, I wish they existed (laughter).

Q: *All your films take place in Madrid. In* Law of Desire, *and* What Have I Done to Deserve This? *you show unexpected aspects of the city. Would other locations be possible?*

A: I think I could shoot in other places. But I live in Madrid and this city is an integral part of my films. Madrid is a diverse city, aesthetically, socially, humanly. There are people who live like in 1940, others like in the sixties, and some like in New York. It's a melting pot of big cities. I think I could shoot in any other city, but I know all the spots in Madrid. With my characters, I draw from many different little details. If I were to change cities, I would first have to live there for a while in order to get a sense for its daily life.

Q: *In* Law of Desire, *the filmmaker is working on* La Voix humanite. *Your next project also has to do with Cocteau's play. What is the relationship between these two plays?*

A: There is a close link between the director of *Law of Desire* and me. People often ask me if this film is autobiographical. I say that it is and it is not. All my films are. I'm behind them all, I talk about what matters to me. I have not personally lived all the situations in *Law of Desire.* What is really particular to me is Pablo's working methods, the way he creates works of art from elements out of his own private life.

While working on the scene from *La Voix humaine* for *Law of Desire,* I like Carmen Maura's role. When I was done with it, I felt like shooting a film version of the play. But, because I lack discipline, I made many changes. I placed the character forty eight hours before the telephone monologue. The basic situation remains the same: a woman is waiting by the phone with a suitcase full of her lover's belongings. But, as I kept writing, everything was fading. All that was left at the end was the desperate woman, the phone, and the suitcase. Yes, I also kept the reference to the title. Since it's "la voix humaine" ["the human voice"] the man's voice is present throughout the film while he is never present. In the original version, you could not hear the voice of the absent one, you could only hear his silence.

Q: *What are your plans now? Are you going to take a break?*

A: No (laughter). I have many plans outside of Spain, but I'm very unde-cided. Maybe an Italian co-production because that way I'll have a lot of freedom working and I can select my own actors and technical crew. I'm working on two stories right now. One is more developed than the other, but I'm not sure yet which one I'll choose. In any case, I'm going to shoot another film this year.

The Politics of Passion: Pedro Almodóvar and the Camp Esthetic

MARCIA PALLY/1990

BY THE TIME *Women on the Verge of a Nervous Breakdown* made a splash at the 1988 New York Film Festival, Pedro Almodóvar—writer, director, designer—had become the preeminent pop cult figure in post-Franco Spain. *Women on the Verge's* ribald kitsch earned an Oscar nomination for best foreign film and fifty prizes internationally. Almodóvar was called the new John Waters, exponent of camp, or sniper satirist in the mold of Rainer Werner Fassbinder. To the latter epithet he replied, "I see the connection: we both like cocaine and we're both fat."

Almodóvar is likely the keenest architect of the camp esthetic in cinema today. Certainly, among those exploring the form, his films are the most visually sophisticated and political, with antifascism, anti-group-think propelling his disarmingly cheeky features. Waters's sense of camp was political, too, in the days of Divine and *Pink Flamingos,* when he was upchucking a revolution against polite repressions and prissy bigotries. But Waters is wading more shallowly these days. His campy replay of the early sixties in *Hairspray* supports a sweet liberalism, a gurgle compared to his earlier crashing rage. His most recent film, *Cry Baby,* is a *Hairspray* redux without the tease.

Fassbinder, by contrast, exercised much of his political ire through grimy realism. Those of his films most ripe for camp treatment—like the 1982 *Veronika Voss,* with its story about an actress friend of Hitler's—confront moral issues head on, lacking camp's sense of cheek. The leading lady of *Veronika Voss* is doped up on morphine: she becomes not a woman ever on the verge

From *Cineaste,* vol. 18, no. 1 (1990). Reprinted by permission of Cineaste Publishers, Inc.

of a nervous breakdown, but one who has broken down and gone to hell. This is *noir,* not camp, which needs more levity and lamé than that.

Almodóvar's work takes the saucy, loving hyperbole of camp and puts it in service of a pluralistic, anti-authoritarian politics. It warns audiences of norms. Creeds of decency—priestly, feminist, fascist, or gay lib—are too crude for Almodóvar's tastes, too literal and neat to explain our appetites. He loathes government and church repression, but also any catechism, from gender roles to manners to the manifestos of well-meaning radicals who would throw over both. "Society is preoccupied with controlling passion because it's a disequilibrium," he said when *Women on the Verge* fell to fame. "But for the individual it is undeniably the only mother that gives sense to life." Political trouble begins, for Almodóvar, when one man's desire is trammeled by another man's clout.

The defense of (unorthodox) libido drives Almodóvar's latest effort, *Tie Me Up! Tie Me Down!* A young man (Antonio Banderas) is released from the psychiatric ward where he was dumped as an orphaned juvenile delinquent years earlier. In hopes of wooing the woman he has loved from afar—a porn *cum* B-movie queen played by Spain's leading peach, Victoria Abril—he kidnaps her in her apartment and ties her to the bed until she discovers that, though he is penniless and a bit loony, she loves him as well.

To make a case for this love, Almodóvar looks to the overblown theatrics of studio-era films and TV melodramas. He exaggerates his plots as they exaggerates theirs. He enlarges the most outrageous passions to persuade us of their importance—to prize our sundry personal fervors against norms of sanity and decent living, legislated or conventional. In a sense, *Tie Me Up!* is a riff on *Beauty and the Beast* and *King Kong,* primers for all tales of unrequited devotion and the humiliations we endure to make our beloveds love us. Like *Beauty and the Beast, Tie Me Up!* suggests that we admit the ties we choose, and that the world respect those who agree to be bound together.

Tie Me Up! is as schematic as *Beauty and the Beast* and *King Kong,* as ritualistic, fantastic, and funny. Like all campy exaggerations, it is too much—from the kidnapping to the bondage to the tropically colored sets, from Abril's swooning resistance to the slapstick to-ings and fro-ings that parade the screen till Abril and Banderas finally make love. Explore the strains of love in a realistic setting and you have Neil Simon; explore them through the fantastic conventions of B movies and soaps, and you have Almodóvar.

In TV and film "trash," desire, jealousy, and revenge expose themselves in grinning leisure, ready for Almodóvar's spotlight. Under it, they grow even more outrageous; they become coming-out parties for obsession. Set on the stage of grand illusion Almodóvar's stars come dressed to kill in living colors of designer kitsch. Emotions are archetypical and played to the height of bathos. Almodóvar's work amply fulfills Susan Sontag's definition in her famous 1964 article "Notes on Camp"—it is epicene, extravagant, theatrical, and fantastic.

But it is without scorn. Almodóvar exaggerates to champion the thing exaggerated, never to demean. His camp is generous and affectionate. In film after film, he draws people unhinged by obsession and makes them his heroes. He leads audiences to admire them in hopes that they will find sympathy for the more modest desires of their neighbors and themselves. In *Tie Me Up!,* Almodóvar sets a scene that is both absurd and disturbing. Yet by the time Abril and Banderas decide to marry, filmgoers are rooting for them. Audiences want them to make it, without the benefits of social workers or cops. Twenty-five years ago, Sontag could look at the state of the arts and conclude that camp is apolitical because it is disinterested in content. In the intervening decades, artists like Waters found the political punch in camp, but none with more persistence than Almodóvar—a child under Franco who came of age during the tarty iconoclasm of *La Movida,* the political and social geyser that shot through Spain on Franco's death.

Almodóvar has done for camp what Woody Allen's generation did for *Yiddishkeit.* He has made of it an international language. Emerging respectively from Jewish and gay ghettos, *Yiddishkeit* and camp began as smart-ass ways for minorities to survive society's hate, to laugh at it. Now, these bittersweet, funny forms are patter for anyone shoring up against exclusion and belligerence, and everyone laughs.

Jews and gays, each in their fashion, milk the trouble they've seen. Hounded for religious beliefs, Jews exaggerate the *tsuris* that comes from being God's "chosen." In a parallel way, gay men, stereotypically dismissed for being effeminate, overblow the heartache of femininity, most pointedly in cross-dressing. Elaborating their woes, Jewish comedians fashioned a comic lexicon for paranoia and martyrdom. (Consider Tevye's query in *Fiddler on the Roof,* "Why can't God choose someone else sometime?") Dolling up their troubles, gay men made a comic theater of abandonment and isolation. Jewish storytellers endure such a gaggle of afflictions that their audiences implicitly ask, so how bad could my life be?—and, in a funny way, are soothed. Analogously, gay men pine: life may be lonely and wretched, but the road was so much tougher for Judy. They too are comforted.

By respecting the soap opera lives of divas and their throbbing emotions, by suggesting all his viewers suffer them. Almódovar has universalized drag. He could never have gotten so far, never have used drag so freely, outside the context of the international gay movement of the last twenty years. Like Harvey Fierstein, he has shown on a broad scale that camp and drag could speak to the world.

Over the past decade, Almodóvar's work has become more precisely drag (and less simply parody or satire). Drag does not call on or embellish real women; it enlarges women who are already distortions or theaters of femininity, like Tallulah Bankhead, Judy Garland, Maria Callas and the rest of the pantheon. Drag exaggerates an exaggeration. When Phyllis Diller magnifies a housewife's plaints, it's parody. When a performer magnifies Diller, it's drag. Ironically, this double embellishment of life's woes tells audiences now how ridiculous they are but how true, how real. Tallulah's tougher-than-thou "ballsiness," Garland's anxiety, Diller's self-derision, and Callas's pathos are emotions anyone might feel but would be too embarrassed to admit, certainly not at such intensity. Drag tells folks to relax, hon, we all break like little girls.

Almodóvar also exaggerates exaggerations, and for the same generous, ironic purpose as drag: to bless out bare, frightening emotions. Sitcoms, soaps, commercials, and B movies are, like Garland, a cacaphony of life's crises. Just as drag performers play off her, an overblown caricature of women, Almodóvar plays off them, overblown sketches of life. In *Women on the Verge,* Almodóvar doesn't embellish the romantic entanglements of the single woman, he enlarges on romance as it appears in daytime TV, already a bathetic magnification.

Women on the Verge begins with a woman jilted by her cad lover who is well on his way to his next conquest. His wife, his exes, his son and all the girlfriends of the jilted woman—complete with heartaches of their own—come trekking through her apartment until, by the end, the film has lampooned every sort of TV soap, including laundry detergent commercials. The plot is a perfect web of clichés, the sets a parade of movie oldies posters. Filmgoers recognize that the stuff of the lampoon is the stuff they've sighed over in earnest (and in private)—the gothic romances and Greta Garbo. *As the World Turns,* Bette Davis, and Bogart and Bacall. Watching *Women on the*

Verge, viewers can come out of the closet—twice: once for the love they make, once for the love they watch. Almodóvar bangs the drum for all night's guilty pleasures, including those on the tube. By celebrating the trash that celebrates our sins, he gives us double absolution.

Almodóvar did not begin with the twofold layering of drag. *Labyrinth of Passions* (1982), *Dark Habits* (1983), and *Matador* (1986) fall closer to simple camp in their rococo embroideries of ordinary—not already exaggerated—*mise en scènes.* The punningly titled *Dark Habits* boasts a group of chain-smoking, dope-shooting nuns with names like Sister Manure who rig up phony miracles to milk money out of believers and support their religious experiences with cocaine. *Labyrinth of Passions* sends up psychiatry's efforts to cure "abnormalities." A nymphomaniac and homosexual discover that they've come to their "perversions" through one traumatic incident with an Iranian princess years before. Once the dreadful moment is remembered, the young people are cured and live happily, and normally, ever after. Also featured are a gynecologist who lusts after his (grown) daughter, and the owner of a dry cleaning store who enjoys a bit of B&D with his daughter, as well. The girls solve their problems by switching places.

In *Matador,* a bullfighter and woman both obsessed with death fall in love and commit the ultimate coitus. The only film where Almodóvar's hyperbole is dark rather than cheeky, it's his most extreme argument for forbidden passion. In the film's last passages, viewers may be stunned by the ceremonious death—or more so by its throttling sexuality. But they also see the uselessness of religious fury and liberal do-goodism. Passion is extraordinary and mysterious. With the slow, winding heat of the movie, Almodóvar lets audiences be fascinated by it and admit its terrible preciousness. For obvious reasons, a persuasive performance by actors Assumpta Serna and Antonio Banderas was crucial to Almodóvar's design. To ensure it, Almodóvar stripped them below the waist while filming closeups of their kiss.

Though convents, psychiatry, and bullfights are institutions where extreme emotions are played out (the mortifications of the cross, the histrionics of the couch, and the rigors of the ring), they are institutions found in life and Almodóvar embellishes them directly. He isn't yet embroidering movies and sitcoms about them. These films champion unorthodox desire, as does his later work, yet they do it without calling up the theatrical forms where those unorthodoxies have already run amok. In 1983, Almodóvar could manage a riff on the convent; later he would have taken on *Black Narcissus* or *The Nun's Story*.

Almodóvar made his move from life to grand trash with the 1985 *What Have I Done to Deserve This?*, which suggests not a satire of a beleaguered housewife but a satire of a sitcom about one. (*Matador*, shot after *What Have I Done*, seems a brief retreat for Almodóvar to his earlier way of filmmaking.) *What Have I Done* features an amphetamine-crazed scrubwoman who, at her wits' end, sells her son to a homosexual dentist and kills her loutish husband with a ham bone which she then cooks in soup. Its frenzied pace makes the film run like a soap on powder, and the close-quarters framing recreates the look of the television screen. *What Have I Done* plays directly off the traditions of daytime TV without quoting any particular sitcom or soap. Later, Almodóvar will lard his films with bits from his favorite movies and television shows. Occasionally, as in *Women on the Verge* and *Tie Me Up!*, he makes up parodic commercials to caricature the ads that caricature the heartburn and neuralgia of life.

Law of Desire (1986) is, to this viewer, Almodóvar's most successful work. Stuffed with plots that would do a decade of daytime TV, it is Almodóvar's raciest drag and clearest politics. Only in *Matador* does he embellish and defend desire as forcefully, and *Law of Desire* has the benefit of being celebratory rather than frightening. His next films, *Women on the Verge* and *Tie Me Up!*, are lighter efforts.

In *Law of Desire*, a gay film director and a younger man fall in love, though the youth is deeply confused about his sexual orientation and keeps exploding in vicious, homophobic rampages that he hopes will exorcise him of his "perversion" and keep his heterosexual cover. The director embraces the young man, even when self-hating rage leads to murder, just as he accepts and loves his sister who—as if the above entanglements weren't enough—is a post-op transsexual who had an affair with her father when she was a boy.

Almodóvar frames his characters' faces with a protective, proud care, and cradles their confusions. Almost like a father, he wants viewers to see how terrific they are, how brave their struggles and good their spirits—especially the joyous post-op, whose happy energy is the best argument for coming out of whatever closet you're in. Her compassion and loyalty are also the best arguments for tolerance. The role is played by Carmen Maura as a cross between Harvey Fierstein and Molly Brown. One also thinks of Craig Russell's irrepressible hairdresser *cum* female impersonator in the 1977 *Outra-*

geous. If audiences can love this wacky gal, surely they can accept the (usually) milder passions of their neighbors and selves—or so Almodóvar hopes. He makes it impossible not to love her.

Compared with the parade of plots above, *Tie Me Up!* seems trifling. Opening on a B-movie soundstage, it immediately announces its campy intent to rhapsodize on *King Kong* conventions. The sets, done in parrot colors, scream "fantasy." What with this awfully sweet guy doting on a supine woman till her love for him awakens, *Tie Me Up!* nearly turns into *Sleeping Beauty.* Lastly, in both Almodóvar's movie and the porn queen's movie-within-a-movie, the girl frees herself and claims control of her predicament, not to mention the guy—which is more than Fay Wray got. If there is a problem here, it's not that the film is bad, but that it's not bad enough.

Yet, *Tie Me Up!* raised eyebrows with its footage of Abril bound to her bed. While the scandalous complexities and bawdier-than-thou humor of earlier films pegged them as iconoclastic fantasies, the relative leanness of *Tie Me Up!* left it vulnerable to literal readings. When *Women on the Verge* was released, Almodóvar said, "In order to use the exaggeration of camp outside its original gay context, you must celebrate it, make an orgy of camp." He had hoped *Tie Me Up!* would be such a celebration, "but it's so stylized perhaps it doesn't come out that way. Perhaps it's not . . . enough."

After the film's premiere at the Berlin Film Festival, he was dogged by questions about rape, most notably from the U.S. press. By making a fable out of force, was he not advocating tying women up, or at least telling guys that's the way to get the girl? *Tie Me Up!* earned an X rating from the Motion Picture Association of America, ostensibly for the love scene between Banderas and Abril—slow, long, and uniquely continuing after the man climaxes—but possibly reflecting the MPAA's overall discomfort with the film. The rating raises quandaries for the American remake, slated for next year, and Almodóvar, who took a bath in acclaim eighteen months earlier, was flummoxed. He sued the MPAA for unfairly casting his movie in a bad light, and lost.

"We are always surprised when we are misunderstood," he said after months of sticky exchanges. "Me, macho—who are they kidding?

"The ropes have nothing to do with violence or S&M. They are a simple— maybe too simple—metaphor for coexistence. Any commitment makes demands on you and limits your liberty. A career or relationship will include things you don't like, but you can't live without these bonds, these ties. You must admit that when you accept a commitment, when you seek it out, you are seeking certain restraints.

"In this sense, my heroine's decision is rational. The guy is hardly perfect, but if she wants his love she must accept him as he is. This doesn't mean that we don't fight to change things in a relationship. But you must know that most things don't change. You measure what you accept until it becomes too negative and then you leave. If you stay, don't lie to yourself. You are accepting the consequences of the commitment.

"I am very concerned with this now. As I approach forty and become more known with more demanding work, it's harder to be open to another person. But if I don't provide that opportunity, I have to be aware of what I am choosing, *preferring*. If I want love and passion, then I must accept the difficulties they impose. I don't demand that everyone be mature in this way; I like people who are irresponsible and impudent. But I can't be. I have to know my choices and do them thoroughly, no matter what the consequences look like to anyone else.

"As for the response to *Tie Me Up!*, we have to be able to talk about what's inside us, even the worst parts. If a filmmaker believed women should be tied up—I don't this is obvious—he has to be able to say that. To censor these thoughts from books or movies is very dangerous. It hides a hypocrisy. Most passions have violence in them , not physical but emotional. It's the nature of intensity. We must not refuse to show that; we must never hide what goes on inside or we will never learn about ourselves."

While making *Tie Me Up!*, Almodóvar hoped its simplicity and clarity would underscore his approach to movies—a sort of squaring off his turf against the Faustian temptations that followed *Women on the Verge*. The Disney studios were especially keen to sign him on, as was the prestigious International Creative Management. (Almodóvar said, "They understand when you want another million, but they don't understand when you say *no*.") Almodóvar declined and returned to Spain to "make something even more personal than my other films." That effort became *Tie Me Up!* "I wanted to assert my independence and control over my career.

"In some ways, I was like the Francisco Rabal character in the film. He plays a well-known director who wants to make a trash movie, but there is such a prejudice against exploitation films that directors of prestige can't do that. When he becomes ill and is physically paralyzed, he decides to do what he wants. In this way he insists on his independence from his friends and fashionable trends, even in the wheelchair.

"I am talking through him, here. I love movies like *Night of the Living Dead, Texas Chainsaw Massacre,* and *Monkey Shines.* They don't have the alibi of being intellectual, like David Cronenberg films [*Videodrome, Dead Ringers*]. I might like to make a B-movie, and even start to think of one. But then, I don't. I make stylized satires, instead.

"It also interests me about the Rabal character that, not only does he decide to make a 'bad' movie that might diminish his career, but he figures out how to use his career to benefit his life off the set. He wants to meet a certain actress so he casts her in his film. She needs some encouragement to get off drugs so he writes a scene where she stands up for herself. In this way, his life and profession are not in conflict all the time, and I want to know more about succeeding in that."

Born on September 25, 1951, Almodóvar grew up in the remote village of Calzada de Calatrava where he felt about as at home "as an astronaut in King Arthur's court." His grandfather made wine; his father was the bookkeeper for a gas station. Pedro read a good deal, painted, and watched movies, especially *Peyton Place,* melodramas with Elizabeth Taylor and Natalie Wood, and films based on the plays of Tennessee Williams.

At seventeen, Almodóvar moved to Madrid where he spent ten years working for the phone company. He wrote for underground newspapers and acted with the independent theater company Los Goliardos. By the time Franco's death released Spain's seething subculture, Almodóvar was at the center of it. He made experimental Super-8 comedies with titles like *Fuck, Fuck, Fuck Me Tim.* He wrote the novel *Fuego en las Entrañas (Fire in the Belly)* and shot a pornographic *fotonovela, Todo Tuya (All Yours).* He led a rock band called "Almodóvar y McNamara," and created the character Patty Diphusa, an international porn star whose serialized confessions appear in the magazine *La Luna.*

Almodóvar made his first feature-length film, *Pepi, Luci, Bom, and Other Girls on the Heap,* in 1980, shooting on weekends and dragooning his friends into reading lines. Its goofy, convoluted script concerns Pepi, who has an affair with a cop's masochistic wife, Luci, to get back at the cop while Luci has a second affair with a lesbian singer, Bom. With a budget of $30,000, *Pepi* became an instant cult hit playing Madrid's best art house in endless runs.

What Have I Done was his first commercial success; *Law of Desire* was Spain's highest-grossing film in 1986, topped by *Women on the Verge* in 1988.

Liking his first results, Almodóvar continued to cast his films with friends from Madrid's club-and-theater circuit. Antonio Banderas (imagine Paul Newman, young and swarthy) was performing in an obscure play when Almodóvar offered him a small part in *Labyrinth of Passions.* Leading roles in *Matador, Law of Desire, Women on the Verge,* and *Tie Me Up!* followed. Carmen Maura, Almodóvar's longtime friend and leading lady, had the starring role in a production of Sartre's *Dirty Hands* when they met; Almodóvar had one line. Maura played Pepi in *Pepi, Luci . . .* and appeared in five of Almodóvar's next seven films, her stinging bawdiness bringing them both to international attention.

Maura and Almodóvar broke in 1988 after *Women on the Verge.* "I am a dangerous director," he said then. "I don't want to sound pretentious but when I work with my actors I become whatever they need at the moment—lover, father, mother. When the shooting is over I separate, and this can be difficult. Actors work with something so deep and private you have to take care of that, but the final morality on the set is to make a good film."

After a year's breach, Almodóvar and Maura "were condemned," as he put it, to meet on the stage of the Spanish Oscars this past March. She was Emcee and he gave one of the awards. "Our fight had become a national problem. The papers were full of articles about us and I wanted to put a stop to it. I wanted a reconciliation."

On stage ("I love the stage, it excites me"), Almodóvar gave her a piece of the Berlin wall and said, "If a wall as solid as Berlin's can fall, I hope the wall between us can fall, too." The paparazzi loved it.

Women center all Almodóvar movies. As in all drag, their appetites, griefs, and manners drive his scripts, and allow Almodóvar to investigate passions that motivate him but which men traditionally mask.

"I am becoming a specialist in women," he says, "I listen to their conversations in buses and subways. I show myself through them. For me, men are too inflexible. They are condemned to play their Spanish macho role."

In notes on his work, Almodóvar has written about his disinterest in the typical screen antihero who, when he loses in love, "leaves his job and good toiletry habits behind and goes on a drinking spree . . . until, finally rejected by the whole world, he resorts to giving waiters hell. I am not saying that men don't suffer or that loneliness doesn't hit us as heavily as it does a woman, but who is interested in making a movie on this subject these days? . . . Women: they are the ones who know how to behave when their boyfriends leave them high and dry."

About *Tie Me Up!,* he added, "It's the triumph of matriarchy, in the best sense of the word. The young man is looking for love and family, but in the last act it's the woman who decides yes or no. She and her sister set the conditions. . . . Women are more practical. In a relationship they work much harder and endure more pain, but when it's over they face it. They know what they are doing.

"The area I come from, La Mancha, is very macho. The women work and don't talk, and the men are gods. But they sit aloof and never get involved with what goes on, so they don't know anything about anything. Women know what people are: this is the ambiguity of the way women lead."

In the end, *Tie Me Up!* is about accepting the conditions of other people's leads. Bosses and lovers set terms; their presence demands our attention and that we change our ways. Ties bind: either we accept them or lose them. In *King Kong,* the girl said no. In *Beauty and the Beast* and *Tie Me Up!,* the girl said yes. Others may not dictate the choice.

Interview with Pedro Almodóvar: *High Heels*

JULIAN SCHNABEL/1992

PEDRO ALMODÓVAR MAKES movies about Spanish behavior. The particularities of his films are as different from those in all other films as the Spanish people are from all other people. The public arrival of Almodóvar's cinematic sensibility in the '80s paralleled the new freedom, anarchy, and general blossoming of the excited Spanish cultural life since the death of Franco. Almodóvar's characters—nuns on heroin (in *Dark Habits,* 1983), parents who sell their son to a dentist to pay their bills (in *What Have I Done to Deserve This?,* 1984), an impotent bullfighter (in *Matador,* 1986), a judge who's a female impersonator (in the new film, *High Heels*)—are the run-of-the-mill citizens who inhabit the high rises of Madrid. Filmed with an eye that impeccably preserves every idiosyncratic detail, with a riotous sense of humor and a deadpan seriousness, Almodóvar's work singles him out as not only one of Spain's great natural resources but an essential voice in movie-making today.

JULIAN SCHNABEL: *Tell me how you named your new film* High Heels.
PEDRO ALMODÓVAR: The Spanish title, *Tacones lejanos,* means the noise of high heels coming from afar—"distant heels." It sounds like the title of a Western, *Distant Drums,* and I like the idea of presenting this movie as a Western, which it isn't. It's a love story of a mother [played by Marisa Paredes] and her daughter [Victoria Abril], but everything happens in a big town, and there is a feud between them.

From *Interview,* January 1992. Reprinted by permission.

J S : *A battle. A gunfight.*

P A : Yeah. It is exactly like a gunfight, between a mother and a daughter. The mother is a famous actress and singer, a very selfish hedonistic woman who has always put herself first. She left her family for the sake of her own success, and her daughter grew up obsessed with her. Fifteen years later, she comes back to perform. What nobody knows is that she is ill and has come back to die in the place where she was born. She's like an animal that sees its cycle as finished. The daughter has tried to imitate her mother in everything and has married one of her mother's old lovers [Feodor Atkine]. There's really something sick about it.

J S : *It sounds like that Joan Crawford film,* Mildred Pierce.

P A : That's a good reference, because *High Heels* is a big melodrama with a parallel film noir story.

J S : *You cast Miguel Bosé as a transvestite judge?*

P A : Yes. On the day the mother arrives, she fears that Madrid has forgotten her, but she sees a wall of advertising with an image of a face that is very similar to hers and the name of a transvestite performer who specializes in imitating her. So she discovers that she hasn't been forgotten after all. That night, they go to see her imitator perform, and later on they meet him when he's a judge.

J S : *Miguel's father was the bullfighter Luis Miguel Dominguin, wasn't he?*

P A : And his mother was Lucia Bosé, who was Miss Italy and then became a very good actress for Antonioni, Fellini, and Buñuel. Luis Miguel was the number one bullfighter. He became very famous outside Spain because he was one of Ava Gardner's lovers. In her autobiography, Ava says very good things about him. When I was writing *Matador,* and thinking of the perfect shape for a woman, I thought about Ava in the period that she was living in Spain.

J S : *Miguel Bosé is a big pop star for young girls in Spain. When I was there and saw you guys, he was wearing a bathrobe and eye makeup and was in total drag. So it's going to be a big shock for these kids to see him dressed like a woman.*

P A : Yeah, it's a big change—I think this new image for Miguel will help them mature very quickly! But he's growing, and, you know, you can't be a pop singer all your life. For me he was like a mutant. Because he's so tall, wearing twenty-centimeter-high heels turned him into a giant—a beautiful one. *[laughs]*

J S :   *Are there any other directors in Spain who you feel are working with a similar kind of attitude to yours?*

P A :   I don't like current Spanish cinema, which is a pity, because I would like to promote it. It's no worse than in France, Italy, or Germany, but we do not have the cinema that we had in the days of Buñuel and Berlanga.

J S :   *I've often felt that your films continue Buñuel's legacy, particularly in terms of humor. It's a reaction perhaps to the oppression I sensed in Spain when I was there in the '70s. When I went back a few years later, I could see there was an artistic revolution going on among young people.*

P A :   Fortunately, everything changed so fast, and in a very natural way. It's like we had been breathing in silence. It was a kind of region without luck. Spain is still a very divided country. But now, since the dictatorship, people mature very fast.

J S :   *Divided between the Fascists and the . . . What would you call the other people, the ones that aren't Fascists?*

P A :   *Los otros?* They are the normal people for me. The civilized people.

J S :   *When I gave a seminar to young painters in Spain, I said to them, "Why don't you look at Almodóvar's films and see what kind of colors, what kind of humor you can find in your paintings?" Those things say a lot about cultural behavior.*

P A :   Behavior has changed very much in Spain, and that is important because it "belongs" to the people and is the only noticeable change. You can't find it in cinema, in theater, in literature. There are some young painters with a lot of humor. But it's the *living* which is important in Spain. All the color, all the liberation, all the humor you find in how people live.

J S :   *Let's talk a little bit about your background. Where were you born?*

P A :   I was born in a small village in La Mancha. Then, when I was sixteen, I moved to Madrid. I just tried to live. I didn't have any money then.

J S : *What was your first job?*

P A : I was an office assistant in the national telephone company. It was around 1969, and I started writing and making movies with a Super-8 camera. That was my only school. In 1979, just on the weekends, I started making my first feature, *Pepi, Luci, Bom and Other Girls on the Heap.* And it was like making a Super-8 film, without paying anybody, with no material at all. And then somebody gave me 50,000 pesetas, and so I made it in 16mm and we blew it up to 35mm. It was influenced by punk, very dirty and funny, in the style of an early John Waters film. And it got banned, of course. After that, I wrote the script of *Labyrinth of Passions* [1982] and then quit the telephone company to shoot it.

J S : *How much did it cost to make?*

P A : A little more than the other ones. Twenty million pesetas—about $200,000.

J S : *Well, it keeps it honest. It keeps it crisp. I guess the problem is when you have to do fifty takes and you're paying a lot of money to do it.*

P A : Now I do fifteen takes sometimes, but I don't want to become an expensive director. For me, the special effects are the faces of the actors and a good line to say. This is as powerful as the thousand special effects of *Terminator 2.*

J S : *What did you do after* Labyrinth of Passions?

P A : *Dark Habits,* then *What Have I Done to Deserve This?* I was successful in Spain from the beginning, but I was regarded as outrageous, like an *enfant terrible.* With *What Have I Done?* I convinced people that, "Well, he is modern, but he has a heart, too." In that film I spoke about my origins, the people who come from their little villages and try to survive in Madrid.

J S : *Are there any particular actors that you want to work with these days?*

P A : Glenn Close is one of my favorites, and I would also like to work with Melanie Griffith. She has something very peculiar, something full of humor, and something morbid and dirty. The idea of working in the United States is something that I have to think about. The main attraction for me is to work with American actors, but I don't know if the production system would fit me well. In Spain, I control everything. I think I would lose something in

America. Anyway, the main thing is just to find or write a script, and then we'll see.

J S : *You once said to me that you trust everybody.*

P A : Yeah, I trust everybody. People always surprise me. And I want to keep it like that. I want to become innocent. I don't mean I'm silly, but it's true that everybody can lie to me with words. It's impossible to lie to me when I'm working. The actors are completely naked.

J S : *I think you also have a way of taking away their embarrassment.*

P A : Perhaps the actors who work with me come with a certain disposition, without prejudice. They trust me very much and I get them to trust in themselves, too, which means they can do everything. They don't have any actual sense of the ridiculous, because they trust that I am looking at them. As a director, I have to have a thousand eyes.

Conversation with Pedro Almodóvar

SILVANA CIELO/1992

Q: *I'll take advantage of your being part of the Jury of the 45th Venice Film Festival to talk to you about your films in general. To start our conversation, I would like to ask your opinion on the figurative culture of the '60s and their influence on your cinema . . .*

A: I became a filmmaker in the '60s and grew up in the period of pop culture. This is the culture I belong to and the culture I use. I identify with it entirely because I lived it in person. I suppose that, naturally, it has a great influence on my cinema.

As an example, for me pop culture is the glorification of all daily objects. And this attention to and love for objects is evident in the manner in which I construct my films. The objects I use for the mise-en-scène of my films have a plastic value and often contain all 'the theory' specific of a film. In my opinion, they have the same value that works of art have for others. I also bring this love of objects into my own life. I don't collect much except for a variety of objects of little value that come from those years. What excites me is the *design* of those objects and the concept of *design* in general.

Pop art is a style that uses color in an unprejudiced, brilliant, and non-realistic way. I consider this "artifice" as something very meaningful in my cinema and as a deeply felt choice. In pop art, objects are what they are but color never belongs to reality. Color idealizes an object and gives it an artificial value I like. I believe this "artifice" in the objects, the walls, the décor, the clothes . . . that reveals and singles out the characters of my films. It also

From *Film Critica*, May 1992. Translated from Italian by Cristina Degli-Esposti Reiner. Reprinted by permission.

completely isolates what interests me most in a film: the story itself and the characters' emotions. The story, the emotions, and the characters stand out inside this absolutely artificial frame. For me, the cinema is representation and artifice.

Q: *I believe that without changing the essential terms or conditions of your poetics from the early films to the latest three—*Women on the Verge of a Nervous Breakdown, Tie Me up! Tie Me Down!, *and* High Heels—*there has been a progressive extension, unfolding, a loosening . . .*
A: Yes, you are right. The tone is more relaxed than before. It's something that comes with age. Do you think this is a flaw?

Q: *No, I find it perfect. I am afraid that others might say that "before" you were making "angry" films and that you have "calmed down" . . .*
A: Indeed, I think that in a more relaxed phase one can say things in a deeper manner. The tone of my films is less "fierce," less aggressive. But, for example, in *High Heels,* the grief, the pain is much deeper . . .

Q: *However, I was referring to the form of the narrative more than to the story being told . . .*
A: In the formal arrangement of a film, as in everything, I follow my intuition and what the film requires of me. In *Law of Desire,* the story, and consequently, its form, is more emphatic, more loudly explicit than in the last film.

Q: *But even then, there was a profound nostalgia . . .*
A: I don't know why *High Heels* required me to express all my asceticism, at least this is what I perceive (laughs). The little bit that I have . . . (serious) Bergman is ascetic . . . It so happened that I brought the sequences to the extreme until, as they say, they would "fall into place" in the editing process. I had never done so many long takes in any other film. I was interested in being the closest I could to the characters, and I was interested in determining for how long I could keep the interest alive to reach the limit, to which I was referring earlier, of when the sequence falls by itself. I cannot explain it exactly, but I was always very close to the characters and I was thinking very little about "movement." There are almost no dolly shots. There are no vertical tilts and I usually move the camera from top to bottom. I almost hypnotized myself at about half a meter from the characters without ever leaving

them, so that I'd listen to them, I'd listen to their breathing and I'd see how their veins would swell up. I would see myself as the interlocutor of the actor. It's a planning that gives the illusion of being classical, ancient, relaxed, but it's exactly what I felt in relation to the story.

Q : *Forgive me for insisting, but I think that one can say that the film does not flow horizontally. There is a lot of movement inside the shots . . . as you say, there is a classical "illusion" . . .*

A : The movement is in the guts of the characters. There is a lot of movement there. I did not want it to become a formal and external movement. I knew I was risking a lot. In the film, there are two killers and I refuse to show them. I wanted to show the reactions of the characters to the dead ones. I deliberately avoided the moments one presumes to be the most dramatic and intense, and I chose what one discards in a dark kind of film. I fled from the childhood of the little girl and from her fifteen years of obsession, and I "reacted" with two very daring ellipses. From the telling scene when the mother (Marisa Paredes) arrives in Madrid and meets the daughter, I immediately jump to a month later when everything has already happened . . . This formal narrative process is very risky because it takes away the most "enjoyable" part of the fiction and leaves the passive one. It lets us perceive how all the action that is not seen has influenced and influences the characters.

Q : *The first of the very few flashbacks of the Victoria Abril character as a little girl is introduced with a splendid dissolve that starts on the background of the airport where she is sitting, it seems, behind the glass, behind the airplanes . . . As far as the shots are concerned, there is the one that recalls David Lynch: the house surrounded by the garden and the trees, the splash of water . . . and then, there is the completely different one of the women's legs that recalls François Truffaut . . . As if these shots were playing with the cinema.*

A : I watch a lot of films. The cinema has become for me a part of my experience. I never cite a film as an homage or a quotation. I cite cinema as if the films I have seen were part of my life and of my experience. Therefore, the shots always have a dynamic dimension as the "citing" of a film becomes part of the script.

In *Women on the Verge of a Nervous Breakdown,* we have the scene of the dubbing of *Johnny Guitar.* I directly steal the dialogue of *Johnny Guitar* and make it the dialogue of my film. And when in *Matador* the two characters enter a theater and see *Duel in the Sun,* I use its image as a premonition for my protagonists. There is always an interaction. I was not conscious of citing Truffaut (in the scene of the women's legs). It was brought to my attention for the first time in France during the first international conference, because in Spain nobody had noticed it. It's an unconscious allusion I accept as active reference. When they pointed it out to me, it made me laugh . . . It also made me happy. It still does.

Q : *The two women have a very deep bond and a deep relationship, but one cannot deny that Victoria has problems with men . . . By the way, in these three last films, the male character, as in* High Heels, *appears with very particular "modalities." He is really never the central figure, but the force of his irruption into the film is great. And, in the final analysis, the films always revolve around his presence. Here you have used that very "particular" sequence.*
A : The male character is the most present when he is the most absent. This is true. It's also true that the murder is a "Lynchian moment." But this film clearly establishes the difference between the way I shot the film and the way Lynch—whose films I love—would have done it. He would have treated Victoria for what she is: a psychopath who reaches an extreme.

Less neurotic than Lynch, with a more Catholic education (laughs) . . . (then serious), I was more interested in making a psychopath become a common person, and I wanted to explain the motivations and reasons that had pushed her to act in a certain way. Instead of detaching her character from the spectator, I try to make the spectator withhold judgment so that she does not have to be forgiven and the viewers can be moved when she is also moved, even while she does horrible things. As they are in the process of buying the rights for the U.S, I would like for Lynch to make an American version of my film and make it his own.

Q : *I have read everywhere that the film is grotesque. There is a difference between irony and the grotesque, and I have to say I disagree. For me the film is ironic. And for you . . .*
A : I agree. It's profoundly ironic but not grotesque . . .

Q : *Like in the sequence where the mother—who is about to die—asks the daughter to solve her problems with men differently in the future . . .*
A : I believe there is a very important, emotional final moment, which is the

gesture of the mother. It does not matter if that gesture counts or not. The mother (Marisa Paredes), who has given nothing to her daughter, has left her a precious inheritance. At that moment, a chapter of life closes. The daughter cannot justify remaining a little girl. She is not Mommy's little girl anymore. She remains alone. Inevitably, that places her on another path (maybe another film). I don't want to say that she will marry the judge, but surely she will have a son and probably she will be a terrible mother because she will love him desperately. For the first time the son will be something completely hers. I'm afraid of thinking about how that child will be. Therefore, the end of *High Heels* is open.

Q: *Just a few, almost obligatory questions about television. What do you think of it? Do you like it? How do you use it?*

A: I'm not a TV viewer. I suppose that TV is something that can make you obsessed with it. I don't watch it regularly because I don't like it. However, it's there. It's part of my furnishings, of the apparatus. It's part of the history of each one of us. I think that with time it becomes a sort of predator of life. Anything that does not appear on TV does not exist. On the other hand, this has a lot to do with the other . . . I also think that only to narrate . . . but the fact is that television is considered more as commerce than as a medium. One traffics more and more with intimate things. On TV, you can see how somebody kills him/herself or another person, or the panties of the girl raped by Kennedy. I don't say this in a critical way, but as a frightened child would. I'm of the opinion that more and more, every day, the most horrible and sensational facts are the most communicable. Pure fiction is the least television-like thing there is. In *High Heels,* television is a sort of confessional place. I like to use places dramatically, to stretch their meaning to extreme consequences. For example, in *Dark Habits* there is a confession sequence. A confessor hears the confession of a nun, and she tells him she loves him. It's the ideal place for a love confession. Victoria is at the telecast news. You assume that the news tell the truth. To talk about the truth is a way to speak the truth as far as its extreme consequences. Not only does she say she killed, but "I have killed and I will explain why." For me, the news broadcast should be a confessional: the telecamera more than the cinema is a great, paradoxical, confessional device. This is all the more true if you think of a woman who works with the televising medium. She tells her tragedy to her only witness, the telecamera, which is like telling it to the whole world and to nobody. It's like expressing in only one sequence the profound solitude of this woman.

Interview with Pedro Almodóvar: *Kika*

ELA TROYANO/1994

ELA TROYANO: *How did you begin writing* Kika?
PEDRO ALMODÓVAR: You mean the script? I began exactly with the controversial rape scene. The novel I was adapting begins with the rapist escaping from the police. But I believe that adaptations need to be "free," you have to keep that original spark of energy, but not be faithful or literal.

That sequence, where someone watches during the rape, ended up being curiously engaging and entertaining, though still a rape. The character of Kika was already present, which is what really stimulated me to continue writing. So, to discover more about this character, I developed the story, completely forgetting about its origin in the novel. In that scene, someone watches, someone videotapes and afterward, what has been taped will be seen on a television screen, which already means two rapes. One is the physical one and the other takes place through the communications media— which is what the film is about. And I believe the one through the communications media is worse. It depends on how—if you want, I'll discuss it later, after all you are a woman. This is not a boutade.

ET: *You use the camera as if it were the voyeur.*
PA: In this age, wherever you find an open window, someone could be looking in. In an era where television is like the eye of god, in this case the eye is a frame, a square frame. It is an omnipresent eye in everyone's life. In every country, any place, there is a television. I don't think there is a day in the

From *Bomb Magazine,* Spring 1994. Reprinted by permission.

year when we don't see an image in that square frame. So, if there is an open window, then I thought that someone with a camera could be watching. From there on I began to depart from the original novel.

Even though what interested me at the beginning was a *comedia loca* and *divertida,* it became something a lot less optimistic than what I wanted. It gets darker at the end and I have not been able to avoid Kika being filtered through what must be my own pessimism toward the life that surrounds me. So, the film has ended up being turbulent, which I suppose is a projection of myself. But these things should not be avoided, one has to be sincere. And that is how I started writing the film.

ET: *Did something on actual television influence you?*

PA: At that time, I'm talking about two years ago, when I was promoting *High Heels,* I had been watching some television programs here in the United States which were not yet "reality shows." There was the Kennedy trial, where one of the nephews was tried for allegedly raping a woman, and you could watch the trial on television. That kind of program really made an impression on me. It bothered me, it scared me. All of a sudden, television cameras could go anywhere. There was no personal space, nothing off limits, even where the police could not go, the video camera could.

And speaking of this woman who had been supposedly raped by a Kennedy, there was a close-up of her underwear, of her panties! And I found this terribly humiliating for her. It's enough to be raped, but that your panties appear on television seemed to me as humiliating as the rape itself. Without the madness, the physicality, it was something much more diabolical. And thinking about these shows I was inspired to make the character of Andrea Caracortada (Andrea Scarface).

Later, as I was writing, I realized that the phenomenon of these "reality shows" was invading all European television. And when I was shooting I thought, I'm too late *(laughter),* what is happening on them has already gone further than what I'm shooting in the film.

ET: *Did you take anything out of the rape scene?*

PA: No. Generally . . . I never censor myself. I mean I am very reflexive when I go to work. How can I say this? I am reflexive technically and aesthetically because a film is something which is quite organized, systematic. A film has thousands of shots. You have to ask for a lamp or you won't get one, you have to ask for a color or you won't get it . . . everything has to be very organized at the time of shooting. But in writing and conceiving the film, my way of being sincere and honest is to have no limits. To let things happen almost from the most irrational point of view. I don't try to control this, much less to be self-censored.

The rape scene is a long scene because the *chico* doesn't leave. He doesn't leave! He wants to break his record for the number of ejaculations. And a lot of other things take place during that scene. But it is shot as it was written. I was actually worried that it would be much more complicated, but the actors worked it out so that it moved fast and there was really no problem.

ET: *Would you like to talk about the style? It seems to me that in every single shot the space is always being broken up . . .*
PA: What do you mean? Say it in English.

ET: *Sometimes a scene begins as a reflection on the water, or is seen through a mirror, or there are so many visual distractions that it is hard to place oneself in a given location. For example, even when you have an establishing shot, like the one with a tree, the tree really acts as a barrier through which we can't see, we can't tell where we are . . .*
PA: It is the gaze of someone who looks without being seen. Someone who looks through things, not only through a window, but one who is hiding and watching. It has a lot to do with our society. We receive images from every place in the world, all kinds of situations, all kinds of peoples, including images which were technically impossible for us to get before. Right now, we can watch how a war takes place on television! We can even watch night-time military maneuvers—think of the Gulf War. We live in a world where we can be sitting down at home and have access to the most intimate, and the most atrocious, images.

And *Kika* is a film that refers to all of this. Everyone watches themselves, everyone is spying on everyone else, and everyone is lying to everyone else. And yet, all of this furtive information about everyone else's life doesn't really help you to understand anyone. It doesn't lead you to help anyone. On the contrary, these images which are seen passively do not move you toward any kind of solidarity with others.

This is something which occurs in our society. We have never had more information about other people's tragedies. I don't believe that we have ever lived in a more alienated world than the one in which we are living now. And this is something which is in the ambiance of the film. But the film is a comedy, and I hope that people laugh, at least in Spain they laugh a lot.

E T :   *The characters seem to reflect this lack of communication.*
P A :   Most of the characters work in the communications field. Ramon is a photographer and plastic artist, Andrea has a television show, Nicholas is a writer. Kika is a parrot, *habla por los codos*. (She doesn't shut up.) And yet, no one communicates. When the characters really talk or communicate, the one they are speaking to is either dead, or asleep, or has fainted. *(laughter)* Paul Bosso speaks to his sister while she is knocked out. He talks to Kika when she is asleep. Kika tells Ramon her life story when she thinks he is dead. Andrea Caracortada has a television show, but she doesn't have anyone in the audience. She shows us the empty chairs. *(laughter)* There is an enormous lack of communication among all the characters. This is something that exists in large cities.

Although you don't see the city that much, this aggressive atmosphere, the hostility of living in a large city is present in the hostile environment in which Kika lives. Kika, a stupendous and positive character, is a *chica* who is a continuous victim of a thousand aggressive acts, from domestic ones to the ones coming from the apartment across the street. The only way in which she can survive all of this is with an extraordinary vitality, which is somewhat the message of this film. That to survive all this hell you need to have an enormously good disposition. *(laughter)* Because if not, you succumb.

E T :   *So how are the characters connected?*
P A :   The action takes place in a kind of labyrinth. All of the action occurs through the windows, the doorways, the hallways, the stairways. I mean, in a way it is an open film where all of the characters are geographically connected. And it is easy to go from one character's window to another character's window, then to the kitchen.

Physically, these locations are related, but not only physically, there are huge round windows that are a metaphor for the eyes and the camera, which link the space—objects in the foreground and the background are seen through these connected spaces. This functions aesthetically and dramatically as what in painting would be called a collage. A number of independent, simultaneous universes are seen together as in a puzzle, which is the dramaturgy of this film—the "puzzle" in which there are many mixed genres which do not seem to be related among each other but which have the same history and universe.

ET: *How does* Kika *relate to your other films?*

PA: All of my films are very eclectic, all of my films mix different genres. I am not a person capable of respecting the rules of any particular style. But *Kika* is more radical than any other. *High Heels* is a drama if it needs to be categorized. In all of them there is humor. *Women on the Verge of a Nervous Breakdown* is a light comedy. I think *Kika* is the most unclassifiable. I don't mean to say that I have invented any new genre, as much as that it is truly hard not only to classify, but to even tell the story. Depending on which character you follow, the story keeps changing. It is the most non-linear. And that always creates a certain challenge for the spectator. That's why I was more worried with this one than with any of the others. The audience likes to feel familiar with what is being told, that it corresponds with their expectations. This is a film which begins telling one story and halfway through the film you begin to discover, with the same elements that appeared at the beginning of the film, that that story is another one, and that it is very different from the one being told. And in the end, you find out it is another story altogether. I don't know up to what point this is disconcerting for the audience.

I see it as a film in which I finish a cycle and where I go toward another, though I don't know yet what that will be. It is a film which serves as a period, an ending to a chapter in my filmography which situates me in another one.

ET: *At the end of the film there is a change in the look, the space is depicted simply, and the coloring is different, full of earthy, almost red blood–browns. Can you talk about this?*

PA: I really love brilliant colors, but here I am using a very different range of colors than what I'm used to. For example, I have never used so many masses of gray. Red is still the predominant color, but in this film there are more intermediary colors than basic ones. Which is still a fairly brilliant coloring, but with more tension or at least, for me, much more drama.

There is a declaration of principles, of the aesthetics with which I work, always based on the *mezcla,* or mix. When I went to Puerto Rico and to Santo

Domingo I said, "These colors are the ones I use, and everyone here used them, on the outside of the houses, in the interiors, everyone uses these colors spontaneously." I feel very close to the Caribbean, which is quite a vast area. The *barroquismo* and the coloring of the Caribbean. . . . At the same time, I was formed by the 1960s which was the time of the birth of "pop." The characters in my stories are very baroque, very expressive. So that mix of pop-barroco-Caribbean, and I don't know, the Memphis furniture style all combined . . .

E T : *What countries have you visited?*

P A : Of these countries, Puerto Rico, Sango Domingo, also I have gone once to Cuba. And I feel very close on a human level to the nature of the Caribbean character and how this nature manifests itself visually, and how it expresses itself through music. Music is something which really defines my characters. The boleros, the mambos that I use in this film, or the trios from Puerto Rico.

I mean, my characters are very *descarados,* bold. They have no shame when it comes to talking about their feelings and they behave in a very direct manner. All of this I find in the bolero. The bolero is a type of song that isn't scared to be tacky. It expresses feelings in a direct way without embarrassment, without shame. In this case, with *Kika,* I used the mambos of Perez Prado. Not only when Kika appears, but also when Andrea appears there is a concert for bongos he composed which sounds very primitive and savage.

E T : *How did you begin to show your work in the United States?*

P A : The Miami Film Festival has been one of the doorways through which Spanish cinema has been able to enter. It is one of the few festivals which features films from Spain. And it is a small door, because the American film industry is not willing to allow Spanish, or any other foreign competition. In the United States, the presence of non-American cinema is about two percent. In Spain the presence of American films on Spanish screens is eighty percent. I am grateful to Anac Seriac, the director of the Miami Film Festival, for being the first to show one of my films.

E T : *Which one?*

P A : *Dark Habits.* And because of the sensation it caused, the next year I was invited with *What Have I Done to Deserve This?,* which was picked up by a distributor and shown at the Museum of Modern Art. Afterwards, I began to be known, and more importantly, exhibited in the United States, which is extremely difficult to do because it is so expensive just to get publicity. Exhibitors don't dare to take films and it is quite difficult for foreign film directors. I came in through the Miami festival and now I am going there for the closing night with *Kika*.

ET: *How do you see yourself as a director in the world arena?*
PA: Films are understood anywhere, they transcend place. The only thing which is of any interest is that films have a personal seal, that they have their own moral, their own point of view, their own *mentalidad*. And that is what distinguishes you from the rest of the directors.

I see myself as a personal director, very independent in every way, economically as well as aesthetically. Although, I tell you, this is really difficult, my films are very Spanish, but on the other hand they are capriciously personal. You cannot measure Spain by my films. I have the impression that I am inventing them, but I am not inventing them from a void. Black humor is at the root of Spanish culture, from literature to painting. And the aesthetics of my films are related to this, but what is really certain is that my films are not like any Spanish films. But in any case, I am a Spanish director.

Spanish cinema is absolutely unknown in the world. I am lucky that I appeared at a moment when Spain was undergoing a great change. And that in the rest of the world, for the first time—at least since I have been alive—there was a curiosity about what was happening in Spain. And a curiosity which was not full of superiority. Spain has always appeared to be culturally inferior. After the democracy, and after it became known that a lot was happening in Madrid, foreigners were coming and saying, what a happy city, fun, free, drugs are permitted. There began to be a curiosity and then my films appeared. I believe it was a juncture that facilitated the connection of my films with the public.

ET: *If your films are Spanish and yet not Spanish, what are they?*
PA: Urban. I am an urban film director. We live in a time where information is shared and alike. For someone of my generation living in the United States, there is a sensibility that makes it seem that we live in the same place, we both use the same references. Lives in large cities really resemble each other. A film made in Madrid is perfectly understood in the United States.

Although I am a well known director throughout the world, I continue to be a marginal director, deliberately marginal. *(laughter)* Fortunately my dreams are not to make expensive films.

ET: *That is what I wanted to ask you next, is there anything you would like to film but which you can't due to financing?*
PA: No. I come from poverty. Socially speaking, my family was a poor family. And also speaking as a producer, a director, my beginnings were *pauper-rimos,* no budget. I'm accustomed to maneuvering myself within a lack of means. That is where I learned to do what I know, that is, if I have learned anything.

To tell my stories I really do not need large sums of money; but to tell my stories, I need an enormous amount of freedom. And control. But I am also aware that I belong to a market. These films, which are something extremely personal, when they leave my hands, go directly to a market and I cannot be so disingenuous as to be unaware of the rules of this market.

The price of my independence will always be tied to my moving within low budget filmmaking. Fortunately, I don't really dream of making fifty million dollar films. It isn't my style. Fortunately, the stories I want to tell do not need enormous special effects. They are based more on great actresses and good dialogue, and that is equal to the special effects in *Terminator.* *(laughter)* For me, two *chicas* talking, two really concrete characters, with a few good lines of dialogue are as effective as any expensive special effects. And they are cheaper. So I will work in this camp.

Interview with Pedro Almodóvar: *The Flower of My Secret*

MARUJA TORRES/1995

HIS ELEVENTH FILM, *The Flower of My Secret,* has left him satisfied and energized, although the later part is nothing new. Pedro Almodóvar is one of the most positive, creative, and ingenious people I know. To interview him is a pleasure, but to write it up is painful when having to limit his witticisms to the space available.

Q: *Let's see if we can manage not to get side-tracked. So I'll ask you a conventional question.*
A: There are no conventional questions; only the answers are. [He smiles, satisfied with the weight of this cliché.] Are you going to ask me about my birth?

Q: *No, I'd ask your mother about that.*
A: You're right. There's a very typical thing about mothers, which is to tell everything from its starting point, its roots. Mine starts from my birth and goes from there.

Q: *Your mother, though she doesn't appear, is very present in* The Flower of My Secret *through Chus Lampreave's character.*
A: I think that this is my most Manchegan film, or rather, the one in which my roots are more present than ever. And I'm the first one to be surprised by

From *El País*, September 1995. Translated from Spanish by Linda M. Willem. Reprinted by permission.

that. They slipped in all of a sudden without me realizing it. Maybe because when I'm inside myself, I improvise very easily. From the moment I decided that Chus was my mother . . . Her character interacts with that of Leo (Marisa Paredes), but since I always improvise a lot with Chus, she always ends up being more than a secondary character. I understand her very well and I adore her as an actress.

Q: *She's our Thelma Ritter, and in* Flower *she's more Thelma than Louise.*
A: [Good-naturedly laughing at my bad joke] Yes, she is as dry as Ritter, because their humor comes from doing nothing with the face. They are fierce, and that's what's amusing, that's what's marvelous. Well, with Chus in this picture I began to improvise, and lots of personal things slipped in. It's almost embarrassing, and I'm also embarrassed that I'm so moved by it. The part that takes place in Almagro, when they are on the patio with that pseudo-Lorcaesque thing of everyone making lace, that I improvised, because I remember La Mancha. And perhaps what I have is a very dramatic version. But from the time I was young I've heard talk about suicides, of people killing themselves in the most frightful ways, because the Manchegan is very hard on himself, right up to the hour of his death. I remember there were suicides from throwing oneself into a well or from hanging oneself from a beam in an attic. And when we were shooting the film, I said to the neighbors, "Listen, did any of your relatives throw himself into the well?" And one woman said yes, and I said "Then, tell Marisa about it."

Q: *For how long did you live in La Mancha?*
A: Was that a conventional question?

Q: *No, although it could have been.*
A: Only eight years, but it allowed me to discover what I didn't want to be, the mentality I didn't want to live with. It gave me the notions I would have to fight against in the future. Everything that I do is the opposite of the upbringing I received there, and nevertheless, I'm from there, I belong to there, with everything that means. And in this film I was conscious of that for the first time.

Q: *I think that's why your cinema is so representative, and at the same time, so different. Because it's a synthesis of what we want to leave behind and what we want to have.*

A: Even to the point of colors. You see, I'm one of those people who thinks it's necessary to have a theory for everything [ironically mispronouncing the word theory] because they're always asking you the reason why you do things. I used to have a theory for when the French would ask me why I use colors—which is what they always ask me—and it was very pretentious, about how as a child I had seen films like *Duel in the Sun,* for example, whose colors were very violent and unreal, and well, I'd say I liked that. But one day I took my mother to El Corte Inglés department store to buy the clothes that she'd wear while reading the television news in *Women on the Verge of a Nervous Breakdown.* What my mother really likes best about working in the movies is that they pay her and she gets to keep the dresses. Well, there she was talking to a salesgirl, and I stayed a few meters away and listened to her saying that ever since she was three years old she had to start dressing in black, including "when I was pregnant with this one" (and "this one" was me), because they would put all of the relatives who died together. And this made a big impression on me, that this woman dressed in mourning was carrying within her a being that was going to express himself in the opposite way. And I guess that is the real reason for the coloring in my films; that I am the result of my mother's revenge.

Q: *But is it to that Spain in mourning that Leo goes when she needs comforting?*
A: Yes, for that type of balm that she finds in the first spot she ever crossed through, the first door she ever had to open. And it is important that the audience knows that this woman who is suffering so much and has to fight so hard had already had her difficulties in being born. The story that Chus tells Leo in the film is exactly how my brother Agustín was born. And your conventional question?

Q: *I think I forgot it.*
A: Did you know that Hollywood is going to make their version of *Women on the Verge of a Nervous Breakdown?*

Q: *Who? Jane Fonda?*
A: Well, Maruja, Jane thinks that at sixty years of age she may not be the most appropriate person to play a pregnant woman.

Q: *Although she's very beautiful.*
A: Extremely beautiful. She's a born athlete. I touched her like this [punch-

ing gesture] to see if she was real. Like a rock! No, Whoopi Goldberg is going to do it, and I really like that they have changed the color of the character. Because the problem they've had with the first adaptations is that they wanted to be faithful to me, and I told them not to be. Because if I take something, from *The Human Voice* by Cocteau, for example—which is what *Women* is—well, nothing remains of the original, except for the essence of an abandoned woman, shattered, sitting on a couch, next to a suitcase filled with memories, waiting for someone to pick it up. So I told them: "Don't respect me, because when I set out to adapt something, I don't respect any-thing." Right now I'm writing the script from a novel by Ruth Rendell, for which I have the rights.

Q : *Which one? I really like Ruth Rendell.*
A : The one about the paralytic.

Q : *Give me the title, because I have Alzheimer's, or rather, a hangover mixed with forgetfulness.*
A : A hangover and forgetfulness? What a great title, especially for a song. Yes, it's *Carne tremula* which in the original is *Live Flesh,* but since that sounded so much like Raphael, the publishing company changed it. As I said, I'm doing the script and, seeing that there's a paralytic in it, and my having also seen five minutes of the Paraolympic Games from Barcelona, I said to myself: why not have him immediately start playing—with all due respect to the disabled—basketball? Then, from the moment that the character becomes a basketball star in a wheelchair, everything changes. Although there continues to be the conflict that interests me.

Q : *Well, let's go back.*
A : To where?

Q : *Truthfully I don't know, but it would be good for you to define* Flower of My Secret *for me.*
A : It's a film about pain, about the growth process.

Q : *And would it have been impossible to talk about something like that using a male protagonist instead of Marisa Paredes?*
A : Let's not fool ourselves; pain is the same for everyone. When you're

abandoned or someone dies, everyone suffers the same. What happens is that women react in a different way, and that's what stories are made of: how people react. Not only are you women more theatrical, but you are also more pro-active. Essentially the story that I'm telling is about this woman's problems in her married life, in her work, in her friendships, in the world, and in all her little worlds.

Q :   *A conflict that is magnificently reflected, cinematically speaking, in the scene with the boots. It reminds me of Billy Wilder's introduction of Jean Arthur's character at the beginning of* West Berlin *when we see her put each tiny object in a little bag, and each little bag into her big bag.*
A :   That's symptomatic of her weakness and of the fact that there are conflicts. Leo knows that what's serious isn't that her boots are too tight, but rather, that the man who once took them off for her isn't there, and she has to go into the street with a spare pair in a plastic bag in search of someone to take them off for her.

Q :   *How was it working with Marisa?*
A :   Very easy. At the beginning, she was not the actress I had in mind [*interviewer's note: Ana Belén and Victoria Abril turned down the role*], and I already had an answer prepared—or a theory, but much shorter—for when they would ask me how I felt about having contracted Marisa at the last minute: that I had discovered late that the script was meant for her. Well, it's the truth. It is for Marisa now. For that reason it was extremely easy. And it's the type of role that can drive an actress crazy, in the sense that she can end up in the hospital, because everything that happens to Leo has to be digested, it has to pass through her, and it is she who has to be willing to take the consequences. I've had cases where actresses have gotten hung up in their roles, and they've told me, "Listen, you have to get me out because you got me into this." However, on other occasions it's the complete opposite: beneficial and therapeutic. What happens is that a director never knows, and that's why I have an extraordinary respect for actors and actresses, because I work with very delicate material. Luckily, in Marisa's case, she told me that she would get up in the morning very relaxed and very happy about going to work.

Q :   *It seems like it's not always that way.*
A :   One thing I've discovered is that, over the last few years, actresses get

very nervous with me. Don't interpret this as pretentiousness on my part, but it's as if all of a sudden an enormous responsibility had fallen on top of them. I keep getting more and more simple, and feeling more and more insignificant, but they still get nervous. Sometimes I have to spend at least two weeks calming them down.

Q: *In what sense do you feel more and more simple? Are you more sociable? More human? More rooted in reality?*
A: How clever you are! All those things. I've never been one to brag about myself, you know me . . .

Q: *I do.*
A: But now I'm much more accessible.

Q: *Nevertheless, people have an image of you as a* prima donna, *and they say that when you are filming you are terrible.*
A: Do you know what happens? It's just that at those times you're concentrating. I see soccer coaches when they're working—the look on their faces—and I see myself as being like them when I'm filming. I don't think that either the coaches or I seem very nice. Because I'm absolutely focused, neither good nor bad, just focused. And that gives you an air of seriousness, of intolerance. But it's just that you are doing something you like so much that your life goes into it. I also have a type of Alzheimer's, as you call it, because when I'm filming, I disappear. I register everything; I remember everything. But I need an enormous concentration for that.

Q: *I just remembered.*
A: What?

Q: *The conventional question. It was: how is the triumphant Pedro Almodóvar of today different from the one who arrived in Madrid wanting to make movies?*
A: Ah, that! Well look, I don't think that I've resolved the essential things in my life. I didn't arrive at my fortieth birthday and suddenly know peace, as generally happens with good-looking guys—although I don't fall into that category—with a past. I'm referring to Richard Gere or David Bowie. All those guys arrive at forty and find peace, and they say so, in different ways. That is, they find an accommodation or a compromise with life that they call

peace. And I haven't found that at all. I think that makes me more and more interested in the small things, the smallest problems, in my surroundings, as well as what I don't know.

Q: *But fame . . .*
A: Isn't good for anything. And that, when you discover it, stops you from putting on airs.

Q: *In what sense isn't it worth anything?*
A: In that the problems that you have are the same ones you would have had if you had remained a bum or if you hadn't been successful. Success allows you to keep working on what you like, or lets you pay for an expensive treatment for a sick relative. And that's it. People get mixed-up about what success means. I don't want to buy anything, nor do I want to buy anyone.

Q: *Nonetheless, it does allow you to make the films you want, that is, to express yourself.*
A: Cinema is my way of expressing myself, and above all, my way of living. But rather than solving my problems, filming allows me to put them on hold. Because Film—with a capital letter—is who rules. It's God. For the sake of a film I'm capable of doing things and making decisions and forgetting problems, which I wouldn't be able to do when I'm not working. But a film doesn't solve anything for you, although it gives you an enormous amount of pleasure. It's like getting laid, which gives you a great deal of temporary happiness, and that's a lot.

Q: *A lot.*
A: Yes, but does getting laid solve a problem for you? For Tía Tula, yes, probably, but after that she could no longer go to mass and live that entertaining life she had had with Irene Gutiérrez Caba, may she rest in peace. Sure, if I were not shooting films, I'd be very frustrated, because I remember, when I was in the administration of the telephone company at a warehouse on San Blas (where they would bring the broken telephones)—I opted to work there because it wasn't necessary to wear a tie—I remember reading *Fotogramas* on the bus. And when I would see the photos of the guys on their film shoots, it wasn't that I felt any resentment, but rather a kind of rage, although it wasn't against them, because everyone who begins something deserves to

succeed, and a film is a very complicated and very hard thing, and they all should work out because it's as hard to make a bad film as a good one. In short, problems—the passage of time, being overweight, loneliness, the lack of love—none of this is solved by making a film.

Q: *Let's go on to the new script based on Ruth Rendell. What will it be?*
A: A type of thriller. I would have liked to have made a comedy, but it's not working out that way. Once again, I'm setting myself up within the realm of desire, and on a bare-bone outline, as it has to be done, with five characters encircled around a theme, but within the thriller genre, which is something I've never tackled before, although there have been a few cadavers in my films. And another thing that I've written is the first draft of a script that will be a Western, and it will be the first time that I will shoot a film in English and do a period piece, to be set in the last century and in Idaho during the height of the gold rush fever.

Q: *A Western?*
A: Well yes, besides, I've been researching the subject a lot, and I found that 150 years ago the United States already had the problems it has today: the blacks were free but racism was brutal; there were many Mormons so intolerance was present; the saloon girls would go to a Chinese man to get morphine to relax after a day of selling their wares; and there also existed the same prejudices that there are now against different sexual orientations. They didn't tolerate them. And in my Western there will be an orientation that deviates from the norm. And how did the settlers get along with the miners living so far from home? There was a feud, Maruja, I'll tell you, and that, though not the main theme, will appear in my film. I'll shoot it within two years.

Q: *You certainly do have an enviable vitality. You are involved in a lot of things.*
A: Did I tell you that I'm also a park?

Q: *A park?*
A: Yes. In my hometown, Calzada de Calatrava, they named a park after me, and I accepted because what it really implies is a homage to mothers. Then I got to thinking how a good park behaves because it's a responsibility that's separate from your decision, as responsibilities are, which is why they are so

bothersome . . . And I wondered what I would do in the future to be faithful to that. It's not that they will take it away from me, but you do find that it is a very pleasant thing to sit down in an open area, even though it seems foolish to you.

Q : *How to survive and perpetuate and all that?*
A : I thought a little about what it would be like to be reincarnated and be a place where people took walks, children ran around, and couples fell in love. But I don't believe in reincarnation, but rather, in reversible things, in what has two sides, in the complexity of life.

Almodóvar's *Secret*

DAVID NOH/1996

IN THE MID-'80S, as the American cinema increasingly fell victim to mindless formulas, a newly liberated Spain gave rise to a string of wild, wonderfully funny and unapologetically sexy movies. Pedro Almodóvar provided a beneficent comic beacon during this dark time and has just finished perhaps his most serious, personal work yet. *The Flower of My Secret,* due in March from Sony Pictures Classics, centers around the compulsively needy Leo (Marisa Paredes), a writer of romantic best-sellers, who finds her entire life a shambles due to—what else?—that old devil, love. Her husband Paco (Imanol Arias) is maddeningly evasive, even cruel; her mother and sister (the equally treasonable Chus Lampreave and Rossy de Palma) are too involved in their own symbiotic sickness to give her any support. This is all familiar terrain to Almodóvar, but this time he explores it with a more muted, subtly compassionate approach that results in an emotional depth beyond anything he has yet achieved onscreen. The director proved himself to be as exuberant, funny, and richly communicative as his work when *Film Journal International* interviewed him a few months ago in Manhattan.

FILM JOURNAL INTERNATIONAL: *This film's theme is romance and obsessive love, a recurring one with you. But it has a more subdued style, with less outrageousness, color and craziness. It really reminded me of those Hollywood movies with Susan Hayward or Irene Dunne.*
PEDRO ALMODÓVAR: Yeah, in Spain the more clever critics said some-

---

From *Film Journal International,* March 1996. Reprinted by permission.

thing similar to that. Curiously, I'm very very fond of that type of movie but I was unconscious when I was doing it that I was making a one-woman picture, like with Bette Davis or Joan Crawford or Dunne or Hayward, where everything is around this big and strong female character. Usually, I'm very unconscious when I'm working. It should be like that—you feel more spontaneous and without prejudices. Those were very good vehicles for women which now don't exist in the industry. There are wonderful actresses—women between thirty-five and forty-five years old, in their full splendor—but no vehicles for them. It's a pity because it's a type of movie that can be melodrama, even comedy, that I like very much, but now we have only action, perhaps because the market is for children. But it's true that our unconscious belongs to that genre, if we can see that. All of my films are very personal, but this is more direct than the others. It is less exuberant, and that was also a challenge for me. I did it because I really felt the necessity to do it, to be very clear to myself, very transparent.

F J I :   *The heart of the movie is the devastating scene when the husband returns. If you've ever had a relationship with all that expectation and then the disaster of what happens, it rings so true. Maybe some would say that the husband was too villainous, too mean from the beginning . . .*

P A :   I think there are very few films made about emotion, not only in America but in Europe as well. We have a need to talk about these things, but unfortunately we don't really deal with these subjects either in cafés or clubs, or in films. I would love for people to talk to me about these things. When I speak of emotions, I speak of authentic emotions, not sentimentality. I don't think the husband is evil. He doesn't really know how to behave because when you face someone like her, that so hurts you, it's very difficult to talk. As men, we don't have that ability to say goodbye and be at the same time a gentleman. Perhaps Cary Grant knows the way, or David Niven, but I don't know if they know how to say, "Honey, I don't love you any more," and be charming at the same time. Also, in my culture, the Latin culture or Mediterranean, the macho behavior really is sunk in. Male characters in real life are used to lying, they lie more than female characters. They say less about their feelings, and at the same time are more practical to face the problems. This film also deals with a very specific state of emotion, which is living in uncertainty. The state that can really drive you to hysteria is when you don't know if the person loves you or not. It's a situation that can last for a very long time. And when somebody abandons you, it is almost the equivalent of somebody dying, a physical loss of that person, as well.

FJI: *The mother and daughter team of your regular actresses, Chus Lampreave and Rossy de Palma, was wonderful, as usual, so funny.*
PA: Chus is one of my favorites. Her role is very important because this movie could be dedicated to my mother and this actress is like my official mother in cinema. It's very moving, what she does. I didn't want to create an ideal mother, I wanted just to make a portrait of a very human and real old mother. The old people I know and like more are very aggressive, not satisfied with living. They always destroy the lives around them. What fascinates me about my mother are not only her good qualities but some of her imperfections, because she is very alive and very funny in those imperfections. And I love this couple, they are funny and so the movie breathes with them. Really, Chus and Rossy together are like a couple of freaks, but at the same time very real and recognizable. It's a kind of gift because they are very weird physically, but together they are Laurel and Hardy making neorealism.

FJI: *Where did De Palma come from? You must have been the first to use her.*
PA: Ten years ago, she had a pop group called the Worst Impossible. They were quite well-known in the very underground scene, but of course she couldn't live on that. When I met her, she was a waitress at this discotheque and she told me she wanted to be in one of my movies. And I said, "Well, of course, you deserve it." At that moment I was preparing *Law of Desire* and I created a small part for her. She was a success in that just because of her image. But after that she understood what being an actress is and she was very interested and very humble and she started studying, learning a lot and making some very different things. Now she's a very complete actress and, with time, I'm giving her different roles with importance in the plot. She's having a wonderful career, modeling for Thierry Mugler and Gaultier, not only in Spain but in Italy, France.

FJI: *I loved her in* Tie Me Up! Tie Me Down! *As a tough biker, she reminded me of Mercedes McCambridge in* Touch of Evil.
PA: Ohmigod! Yeah, yeah, yeah! If one day I make an ancient Roman epic like *King of Kings,* she would be perfect for that. The bitchy makeup and hair

then is perfect for her: She can be a queen or a slave or Egyptian. I don't have any script of a Roman epic. We call those movies "peplum."

FJI: *Marisa Paredes had almost a Garbo quality at times.*

PA: That was intentional, in my very humble way. Those type of Garbo hats and big glasses fit her well. I wanted a kind of anonymous appearance, but anonymous like Jackie Kennedy or Garbo. They can almost be confused with the crowd, but when you look at them, they are gorgeous in those clothes, the most perfect way to pass unperceived, but with enormous class. There is, particularly, her scene in the bar where the more distraught and destroyed she seemed, the more wonderful she looked. It reminded me of Garbo's greatness. There is a quality in Marisa that I admire very much in this film and it harks from that mysterious quality of Garbo. She also has sort of a visceral quality of the Tennessee Williams characters, like Elizabeth Taylor in *Cat on a Hot Tin Roof,* that mixture of being open and torn apart, with style and guts. This mixing of the guts of Taylor with the spine of Garbo is very interesting. I don't know if she's successful now, but in America you have a *wonderful* actress, who also mixes these two things in very sincere and passionate acting, Gena Rowlands.

FJI: *I don't speak Spanish and I always wonder about the subtitles. Do they really translate what you're trying to say?*

PA: In all of my movies, but especially this one, each character speaks in a different way. Fortunately, you loved the mother because she speaks in one impossible Spanish, not academic at all, a really old and very specific tongue that belongs to a small region of Spain. The men speak in a completely different way, very rude, a language that comes from the South. All that makes the characters richer, and it all disappears with subtitles. This is always a big limitation because I can't avoid using language as part of the characters. All my movies lack 30 percent when they are shown dubbed or with titles. I'm very surprised that they can be understood at all. *Women on the Verge,* the most successful movie I did, had that character of Candela, played by Maria Barranco. She was a model and, in Spain, that role became the big revelation of one actress. At that moment, she was one of the biggest actresses in Spain, but that role was not understood outside of Spain because she talked with one impossible and very difficult Spanish. All of the actors became internationally successful (Rossy, Antonio Banderas, Carmen Maura. But Maria Barranco was only okay outside of Spain. I saw then, very clearly, the weakness of subtitles. Of course, it was understood that she was engaged to a terrorist and he was using her, but it was the way she said everything. In Spain, people would laugh the minute she opened her mouth.

F J I : *One thing that I did get in your new film, however, was the reference to your "rival" director, Bigas Luna.*
P A : You know, I used his name because I think he's the only one who didn't mind to be called there, and he has no prejudice and I'm sure that he sees that there is no malice on my part. I think he's the only one who speaks very well about me, because my fellow directors, you know, give me no support.

F J I : *You are such a starmaker, what with Rossy, Carmen Maura, Antonio . . .*
P A : Oh, yeah! And then he becomes a bigger star than me! It's wonderful to see people that you used to work with become so big. It's a very positive sensation, gives me the feeling that I give good luck to them.

F J I : *Some of our TV stations showed you with Banderas and Melanie Griffith in Madrid. That must have been a wild experience.*
P A : I like her very much. Melanie has something that I like most in American female acting, a quality of the young Shirley MacLaine or Judy Holliday, with the ingenuity of a Marilyn. I think she's a very good dramatic and funny actress, but she's wasted because nobody writes a role for this girl. This is all good for them; they are really, really *completely* in love. It became like national gossip, so it was important for Antonio. I think this is the only thing he needed because he's really becoming a big star. For me, it's difficult to talk about that because this is the only actor that I miss in Spain and he's better than he thinks. I think he's doing exactly what he wants so he's not mistaken, but for my side, I'm not interested to see him in these action movies. But he likes to do them, so it's good for him. I can't judge him, but he's much better than that. There are not many actors who could do what he did in my films. But, in any case, what he's doing now is a myth because no other Spanish actor has gone as far as he has in so short a time. I think, with time, he will need to go back to do other types of movies and I will certainly be there to direct him in them. But also I know that right now is not the moment. I hope that he goes very far and very high but really very low in poverty, and then I will go and rescue him.

F J I :   *Bravo! What about you working here? Has Hollywood called?*

P A :   Yeah, every month I'm sent one script. There is always the possibility. I'm learning and improving my English but I want to be very sure that I can do it and the language is not a problem, explaining to the actors what I want. But there is something in the way of production here that doesn't fit me very well. It's not a question of power, but I'm involved in every small thing in the shooting and here the director is just one part of the shooting. It's not the way I learned to work, so I don't know if I could do it or not. I'm sure that I'll do one movie in English, I think I prefer just to deal with one European company and after to have American distribution. I think that I would feel more free. Jane Fonda's company wanted me to direct the American version of *Women on the Verge,* or do the script adaptation, but I was not interested. I liked very much the idea that they wanted to make the movie. I felt like Tennessee Williams, to be adapted into different languages, to think that one script can generate something new, but I don't think it's a good idea to be involved in that. Also, when you ask for the rights to something, you want to be completely free. That was the first thing I told them: Make the adaptation you want, don't try to be faithful. You have to be inspired by art, don't translate word by word. It seems now they're going to shoot it with Herbert Ross. The role of Carmen Maura is supposed to be done by Whoopi Goldberg, and also the role of Julietta Serrano, the old lady who became crazy, is planned for Paula Prentiss. I don't know if you remember her; I loved her. To think that the American version could be the comeback of Paula Prentiss, wonderful! You know, they offered me *To Wong Foo,* but the screenplay was *awful.* It was a fairy tale of drag queens, like "Let's do something about this subject but without telling *anything* about the subject." The plot was impossible, there was no pacing at all. It was really almost insulting. I even met with Wesley Snipes in Miami and I couldn't imagine him as a drag queen. I'm curious to see it.

F J I :   *You were twelve years working with a telephone company, which is interesting because there are so many people who dream while they're working at very mundane, boring jobs. What kept you alive when you were doing that?*

P A :   Really, my story is almost a lower-level melodrama. I mean, a boy who comes from a little village trying just to survive and all these kinds of things that happen only in movies. It's an impossible story but it happened like that. It is a surprise that I'm making movies, because in my case it was almost impossible to dream of that. I was not born in the right place in the right family in the right town in the right language or in the right moment to make movies. But I did, so it's like dreaming of being a bullfighter when you're born in Japan or England. But it was so clear for me, there was an up side to it and it gave me, since the beginning, a kind of direction in my life. I could avoid other temptations in my mind because it was very clear what I wanted to do, but now I'm conscious that it was a kind of miracle. Everything, all my energy I gave to this work and when you have such a vocation and you are seriously generous to that, I think you'll get in. It doesn't mean you can get just in if you want and everything's possible. No, it's a question of balance. I wanted to be a storyteller, I just wanted to tell stories with images in movement, Super 8, 35 mm, whatever. And I started doing it when I could. Before making features, I made ten years of Super 8 movies just with one small camera. For me, *that* was to be a director, not to go and be nominated for an Oscar in Hollywood.

Pedro Almodóvar: Spain's Freest Spirit Gives Maturity a Try

CELESTINE BOHLEN / 1998

AT FORTY-SIX, Pedro Almodóvar is no longer the overgrown kid he was back in the early 1980s when he sprang from the thick of Madrid's anything-goes night life, armed with a hand-held camera, to record the intoxication of Spain's post-Franco freedoms.

Funny, outrageous, sexy, even kinky, his early movies had plots that veered off at random angles. Culminating with the wackily exuberant *Women on the Verge of a Nervous Breakdown,* which won him international acclaim and an Academy Award nomination in 1988, they were a reflection of their author's disheveled, carefree life. "My first films coincided with a moment of absolute, vital explosion in this city," said Mr. Almodóvar, whose hair is more neatly shorn than in his wilder days but still stand up on end, giving him the look of a startled teenager. "Madrid in the beginning of the 1980s was probably the most joyful, the most fun, most permissive city in the world. It was really the rebirth of the city after such a horrible period as the Franco regime. If there was something characteristic about Madrid, about the culture of Madrid that I belonged to, it was its night life. That was my university, and the university for many others."

Mr. Almodóvar, the most visible exponent of "la movida," as the cultural ferment in Madrid after Franco's death in 1975 was known, had arrived in the capital in the 1960s, a teenager escaping from the stifling, strictly Roman Catholic environment of the region La Mancha. In the spirit of the times, he tried a bit of everything: he created comic strips, performed in a drag act, sang in a rock band and worked for the telephone company, filming his first experimental movie on weekends.

Sitting recently in a modest office at his production house, El Deseo, surrounded by film posters, books and a few odd, kitschy mementos, Mr. Almodóvar was ready to admit that he had grown up, if belatedly. And his twelfth film, *Live Flesh,* which opened on Friday in New York, is, in fact, a reflection of the adult in him, with a more sober look at love and passion and even a sidelong glance at the yearning for children and family.

Based very loosely on a novel by the British mystery writer Ruth Rendell, *Live Flesh* is the story of five characters—two women and three men—whose lives are linked by a shooting in 1990 and the accompanying elements of revenge, desire, and jealousy that reach into the next several years. This is a typical mix for Mr. Almodóvar, but unlike his more freewheeling films, *Live Flesh* stays on a fairly tight track as its plot unfolds.

In this movie, as in most of Mr. Almodóvar's others, Madrid itself is a major protagonist. But this time, the city—like the director—has lost its glitzy surface. The Madrid of *Live Flesh* is not the highly colored, highly stylized skyline seen beyond the penthouse in *Women on the Verge;* it's a gritty place of forgotten shantytowns and kindergartens for needy children.

In Europe, critics have hailed *Live Flesh,* which opened in the fall under its Spanish title *Carne tremula,* as a welcome departure from the director's old formulas. "The protagonist of the 'movida' has learned how to structure both his stories and his emotions," concluded a review in the Italian newspaper *Il Mesaggero.*

"I am not sure where he is going," said Ángel Fernandez-Santos, a film critic for *El País,* the Spanish newspaper with the largest circulation, in an interview. "But I think Almodóvar is entering his period of maturity. He is starting to show complete command of the art form. The earlier films were interesting, but they had little mistakes. In *Live Flesh,* the whole puzzle fits together."

Mr. Almodóvar hates putting labels on his work, but he admits that both *Live Flesh* and his 1995 movie, *The Flower of My Secret,* about a romance-fiction writer with a bad marriage who starts writing under her real name, are departures. "In the last two films, I was attracted to narratives that were much more austere and sober," he said, "but that was because that suited those stories best."

He paused briefly, then made an offhand confession. "It also may be," he said with a smile, "that I am saturated by myself, by the things that I have done in the past."

Two of the characters in *Live Flesh* are trapped in a love that is violent and self-destructive, always a subject of fascination for Mr. Almodóvar. But the main protagonists are two attractive young people, Victor (Liberto Rabal) and Elena (Francesca Neri), who experience a more innocent, albeit very complicated, romance.

At the start of the film, Victor's birth, on the night in 1970 when the Franco regime declared a state of emergency, is shown, in the back of a bus on a grim, empty Madrid street. By the end of the movie, Elena is about to give birth to their child in the back seat of a taxi as it drives through brightly lighted downtown streets that are buzzing with shoppers. These two nativity scenes serve as bookends, not only for the movie's interlocking love stories but also for the country's historical trajectory over the last quarter-century. And it is here that Mr. Almodóvar returns again to reaffirm, and celebrate anew, the meaning of freedom.

"The two protagonists in this case have a happy ending because the happiness is the realization that the human being who is about to be born will be born in a better country," he said. "All my movies have a political commentary imbedded in them, and that is the freedom that the characters enjoy."

"I truly think this is the only country where I would have been able to do the things that I have done," he added. "I don't think I could have done them in England, France, or the U.S. This is a free country where I can work in complete freedom. And in Spain, we hold on to our freedom like children clutching their most precious teddy bear."

But for Spanish audiences, Mr. Almodóvar has dropped an ominous note into the narrative: the voice heard on the radio announcing the state of emergency belongs to Manuel Fraga Iribarne, the president of the Galicia provincial government who was Franco's minister of information and went on to become the grand old man of the conservative party that rules Spain today.

"There is a ghost on the horizon, and that upsets me like it upsets many Spanish people," said Mr. Almodóvar. "I think it is impossible for Spain to go back to that awful past, but we are not so far from it either. That voice on the radio is still a live voice; it belongs to an active politician who in fact created the party that is now in power."

Mr. Almodóvar's relationship to his native country is fraught with ambiguity. He is treated like a superstar—the premieres of his films are always top social and cultural events in Madrid—but his peers have yet to vote him a Goya prize, Spain's top cinematic award.

"There is a kind of tradition here," he said, when asked about the absence of *Live Flesh* from this year's list of Goya nominees. "There is a huge hostility against me that is demonstrated every year at this time. I was too successful here and outside Spain. It is a question of envy."

Although he remains committed to the city he calls home, Mr. Almodóvar laments Spain's eagerness to join ranks with its northern European partners. He thinks this policy has spawned a deadly homogenization, forcing Madrid to trade in some of its Spanishness—its late hours and its siesta, for example—for the sterility of, say, Oslo.

The Madrid in *Live Flesh,* he says, could be any city. "I wanted to show a contradiction, both architectural and social, a contradiction which is very alive, very expressive, and very unjust, the kind of thing you see in every big city today."

There are also economic pressures peculiar to the 1990s that have changed his beloved city, by putting a premium on competition at the expense of creativity. "Young people now are very preoccupied with the market, which is natural," said Mr. Almodóvar, still a hedonist at heart. "But I remember in the early '80s, everything we did we did for pleasure, because we liked to, for the joy of doing it. Now people are not doing that, and it is a pity. Because, when you are starting out, that is when you need to do exactly what you want, with no responsibility."

Almost All about Almodóvar

ALICIA G. MONTANO/1999

Q : *Family is a constant in your cinema, and I'd even say in your life. In* All about
My Mother *various characters of yours end up forming a family, albeit an atypical
one.*
A : Family is essential, and if you don't have it, you look for it, you begin to
form it throughout your life. The family of the next century will be an emotional nucleus composed of two women, or two men, or a woman and a
man. And the children will be from both of them, or one of them, or none
of them. The family fulfills a role, but that's no reason for me to stop recognizing that it's a primary instrument of repression. No one can blackmail
you so well, so brutally, and so painfully as the family. I believe in the family,
although I was forced to leave home so my father wouldn't send me to the
Civil Guard because I was under age. But I didn't want to stay in my village,
and little by little they began to understand that they couldn't plan out my
life according to theirs.

Q : *Is it true that in your house they used to ask themselves who could this boy
have taken after?*
A : They looked at me like an extraterrestrial because I even liked to read the
1950s brochures from the Corte Inglés department store, which were lovely.
I always asked for books from the Reno collection, and it was all the same to
me if one by Morris West came or another by Herman Hesse or by Françoise

From *Fotogramas & Video*, May 1999. Translated from Spanish by Linda M. Willem.
Reprinted by permission of Fotogramas, Comunicación y Publicaciones, S.A.

Sagan. The boys around me didn't read that much, and in my home they didn't know who I took after. Later, when I came to Madrid and I showed them that I had enough strength, courage, and initiative to fend for myself, they began to say: "We don't know the kind of life he's leading, but it seems to be good enough." And they started to calm down.

Q : *In* All about My Mother *there is an implicit homage to motherhood. Is father-hood just as important to you?*

A : There's this erroneous belief, which is the assumption that the desire for motherhood is something feminine. But we men also need to be fathers, and we need it in an irrational way. It's something very important, and for that reason in the film I defend the right to fatherhood for the most evil character and the one who has caused the most harm, because it's possible to be self-centered, not to think about anyone else, and—with or without breasts—to want to be a father.

Q : *Have you seriously ever considered that?*

A : Many times. I've thought very seriously about finding an appropriate girl and having a biological child with her. What happens is that in my case, the idea is to have a child, not a family. On the other hand, I'm neither all that crazy, nor all that young. And you have to think about the kind of life you are going to give this child, and how you would be able to take him or her to film shoots.

Q : *Speaking about family, you never talk about your two sisters.*

A : Well, we see each other a lot. Their names are María Jesús and Antonia. They are two typical housewives from Parma, but very open-minded, mod-ern. They are two ordinary women, married, one to a *Guardia Civil* who died three years ago, and the other to a metal worker. I come from a family of humble origins, but liberal by nature, and we are very close. Besides, when my father died, he made me the head of the household, and I act accord-ingly.

Q : *When Roberto Benigni picked up his Oscar, he thanked his parents for his poverty. Could you tell me what advantages it has?*

A : To be born into a family with economic difficulties makes you look at life objectively. It helps you to understand the meaning of the great adventure that remains for you to live. I've always been aware of the things that pertain to me: my sexuality; my economic situation; the work that I like; the people that end up being my executioners. I've been through difficulties, but I've had sufficient strength to fight, and if I have to do it again, I already know how it's done.

Q: *Isn't it exhausting being self-taught?*

A: I don't give it the least bit of importance. Besides, I don't like people who complain about the circumstances into which they were born. I'm self-taught in the sense that I've never gone to a film class. I think that cinema can be learned but not taught. There are very few rules, and they are learned quickly. The rest is just how you look at the story. That's the difference between one film and another: the director's point of view. Really, it's a moral question.

Q: *In* All about My Mother *you highlight a line from Truman Capote's* Música para camaleones [Music for Chameleons]: *"When God hands you a gift, he also hands you a whip; and the whip is intended solely for self-flagellation." What is yours?*

A: Probably, I suffer excessively during all of the creative phases of my films, and since work is the most important aspect of my life, I should try to fix that. I don't want sabbatical years. For me, the great adventure is to go on discovering characters and giving them shape. But I have a terrible time alone when I don't know what I should do. It's like being on a safari, but at home. That's one of my crosses. The other is age. I have a real problem because I'm not taking it well. I think like a twenty-five year old kid; I continue to have the same curiosity, but my body, in effect, is not the same. And, in terms of Capote, I chose that line because I believe that no one has talked about what the act of creation is as accurately as he has.

Q: *In the film it's the mother who, as in an initiation ritual, reads the preface to* Música para camaleones *to her son.*

A: That scene moved me a great deal. Actually, it's one of the texts that I had selected for my mother to read before the camera in a film that I have always wanted to make and now never will. Basically, it would consist of putting a camera in front of her so that she could talk, because what she needs to do is talk and tell stories about things, and she is very entertaining.

She would read—something she does very well—a series of texts. She would be this mother who is teaching you what's best. I remember in *Live Flesh* the mother tells her son: "I'm going to teach you what's best," and she teaches him to fuck, which is a very important thing for a boy to know, if you can get rid of that prejudice in your head.

Q : *Do you realize that a synopsis of your film is impossible: a woman made pregnant by a transvestite; a son who dies while waiting for an actress; a lesbian diva hooked on a young heroin fiend?*
A : The synopsis reads like a serialized novel with innumerable installments, but nonetheless, to me, the author, it seems that the plot is an ordinary story, even though what is told is very powerful. I always believed that if the actors correctly carved out their characters, the audience would end up seeing La Agrado or Lola, the transvestite father, as they are, that is, as a father and a woman like any others, despite how they appear on the surface. For several months we lived within the transvestite environment, with their parallel lives, and all of them ended up seeming quite normal to us.

Q : *What's the secret to making the extraordinary seem commonplace and believable?*
A : I think that rather than tolerance—a word I don't like because it implies a moral judgment—the key is a narrative naturalness, and I'm using naturalness in the philological sense because I tell stories of situations that pertain to nature. Everything that is told, no matter how outlandish it may seem, has a reading that brings you closer not to Manuela, or to the nun, Rosa, or to the professional transvestite, but to the mother or to the father who, no matter how many breasts he has, wants to know the child he created.

Q : *And to what extent have you given legitimacy with your films to the different forms of sexuality?*
A : I've never wanted either to demand anything or to call for solidarity, because that's admitting that there is something that needs to be excused. I've always preferred to tell these stories more than to go to a rally to vindicate something or other. I know full well that there are times when people pay a tremendous price for having a different sexual orientation like homosexuality, or for practicing transvestite prostitution, or for changing their sex, or for needing to have an abortion. And if these people already pay an

enormous price, and if life already charges them more than they are going to receive in return, who are we—the rest of us—to criticize them?

Q : *The character La Agrado (Antonia San Juan) is based on a transvestite you knew . . .*

A : La Agrado was one of the first transvestites that I met twenty years ago when I went to Paris for the first time. There were lots of girls there, especially from Andalucía, who had arrived as men, leaving their families at home, married, with children. And right away, in less than a year, they had breasts that were bigger than the ones their wives had. Indeed, they worked harder than anyone, in the best houses in Paris, and when referring to the money they made, they would say: "All for Spain, all for Spain." And I remember that some never changed either their wives or their lives. La Agrado was marvelous and they called her that because she was nice to everyone. When I knew her, she was already older and devoted herself to initiating the younger ones, as if she were their aunt. I hope that she's still alive and feels that a tribute has been paid to her. It's curious, because the most outlandish and exaggerated characters in the film—La Agrado (Antonia San Juan) and Lola (Toni Cantó)—were inspired by real people.

Q : *Who was Lola in reality?*

A : There was a Lola, with another name, in the Barceloneta. He had a wife, whom he wouldn't allow to wear a bikini, and yet, he would walk around with two breasts like two big wagons, throwing himself at any guy that he could. It's the best example of what machismo is: something irrational, like all the big stuff that happens to us, like racism, paranoia, or not making any sense.

Q : *Was it difficult to come up with the morphologies of La Agrado and Lola?*

A : They were complicated characters with uncommon physical characteristics. In the case of La Agrado, it was luck that Antonia San Juan already existed. What happened is that Antonia is younger. I wasn't sure about her, and I subjected her to three weeks of tests. Besides, she dressed very simply, like a Japanese woman, and the first time she came to see me, she seemed like a nun. But she slimmed down. We made her look divine, although occasionally she did look like a monster, but that was in the kind of scenes that actresses are grateful for. And finally, I was convinced that she was superb.

Q : *The character of La Agrado is like the oxygen, the life breath of the film.*
A : I think her function is to console the viewer somewhat. Her life isn't anything to rave about, but her attitude is. She is so optimistic that she always finds a silver lining in everything that happens. She can't be beaten down.

Q : *Are you satisfied with Toni Cantó's transformation as Lola?*
A : It was hard for him, and he had to be subjected to the torture of tiny belts and bodices, because a man's bulk, no matter how slight it may seem, ends up being excessive when he becomes a woman. I wanted him to look like someone who is sick but still desirable, to men as well as women. When we tested the other candidates, I would ask my actresses, "Would you be attracted to them?" And they would tell me "Yes" or "No," depending what they thought. But when we tested Toni, they mostly said yes, that they would be attracted to him.

Q : *Are you aware that you have released a film of grand emotions and many tears?*
A : Those who cry will reap the benefits because tears are relaxing: they cleanse you; they comfort you. That will always be better than what happens to me: the film puts a knot in my stomach, the permanent sensation of having a very dry cough, wanting to spit and not being able to. *All about My Mother* turned out to be very painful for me.

Q : *Nevertheless, the moral is that there always is a reason to fight and not give up.*
A : It's not a sad film; there aren't any sad characters. It's a film about women with a tremendous amount of energy who spend their lives struggling. Even though they may live through extremely difficult situations, they fight like real lionesses. Manuela (Cecilia Roth) isn't sad: she's destroyed, as if she had been charred by a lightning bolt. She's not a woman who can be wounded; she's almost a zombie; she's debilitated, and nevertheless, when life rips her apart again, she doesn't know how to deny herself any longer and she ends up unleashing all of her love for her dead child.

Q : *In* All about My Mother *there are lots of extreme situations. Why do they turn out to be so effective?*

A : It's not just a question of being effective. In desperate situations people become more generous; they are better disposed to those like them. When you believe that your situation doesn't have a solution, you become more spontaneous, you get involved in the lives of others, or if you like, in the dangers of others.

Q : *Your film reminds me of Russian dolls and those Oriental tales where everyone ends up being in the same place at the same time.*
A : In real life, chance can be within oneself, but in fiction it is imperative to bring together, over the course of an hour and a half, people who normally would take years to get together. It's not so much coincidence as it is the possibility that we have to find ourselves with people or circumstances that we think we have left behind. But, yes, it's true that my film has a circular narration and that the epicenter is Manuela, a woman who spends her life running away: first from a man named Esteban, and then from the memory of his son with the same name; who flees from his father and then returns to look for him; who is persecuted by Tennessee Williams's *A Streetcar Named Desire* as if the streetcar were a wild, fierce animal that rips her apart and is present at all of the important moments of her life. She runs away but can't overcome the attraction she feels for things that are stronger than oneself and against which one cannot fight.

Q : *Do you think that life offers as many opportunities as the movies?*
A : Life ends up being almost shorter in real life than in fiction. Still, I do believe that it gives us opportunities, although it usually gives more to those who are adventurous—to the crazy people who play with their lives, who place bets on their decisions—than to those who carry out an organized and ordinary existence.

Q : *How much does* All about My Mother *resemble the film that you originally had in mind?*
A : It fits pretty well with what I wanted to do. The thing is that I'm not really connected to my films when I finish them. The other day [he's refer-ring to the first screening with the entire cast and crew] was the last time I saw it. As of right now, I no longer have an opinion. Even at this very moment—other than the things that I remember having strongly affected me while I was making it—I'm just repeating what I've heard. The editing

process grinds away my entire ability to be a viewer. What I can tell you is what I remember from before the editing, the sensations that affected me, the tough scenes, the ones that touched me emotionally . . . But I have to do all of this by using my memory because I no longer see the film in the present tense. It's a shame because I can't be a viewer of my own work.

Q: *Will you end up giving in and taking it to the Cannes festival?*
A: I don't like to take films to competitions. You already compete enough, in a natural way, at the box office. The film is sold everywhere, and I wouldn't mind going to Cannes and having a *soiré* if they accept it for the official session outside of the competition. But I don't want to compete. And I swear to you that it's not for fear of coming out badly. It's just a case of not wanting to go to war.

Q: *When they gave you the Silver Ribbon, the Italian Oscar, for* Live Flesh, *you said that the Italians were fortunate because they had a Minister of Culture who helped the cinema, which doesn't happen in Spain . . .*
A: Walter Veltroni knows a great deal and is very nice, but Roberto [Benigni] already told me that he didn't have anything to do with it because they had stayed behind to take a vacation in Tenerife . . . I have no doubt that Rajoy's intentions are good, but since two such complex activities as education and culture are dealt with together, it makes me think that they are treated with a certain lack of personal interest.

Q: *Have you decided yet if you will film* The Paperboy *in the United States?*
A: I have a month to figure it out. The script of Peter Dexter's novel is already written, and I like the story. What's happening is that I'd have to go to the United States, to film in another language, and some days I think I'll do it and others I think not.

Q: *And is that comedy ready that, according to you, wasn't coming along too well?*
A: I think that the next one is going to be a comedy about housewives in economically limited situations, in the environment of the slums, miserable. Women with initiative who—since the thing that they know how to do best is cook—end up opening a restaurant that works out very well. It's a film

about the hell of housewives in very precarious situations, with the tone of *What Have I Done to Deserve This?* but in a more impoverished environment.

Q: *Before we finish, tell me how things are in your personal situation, if you are emotionally calm or if you are restless.*
A: Emotionally I'm very busy. I always try to have an emotional complication. There are two moments—when I get to a hotel and when I arrive at the airport to go back home—in which I need someone to call. I can go to my home and be alone—which is how I live—but when I arrive at a hotel and leave an airport, I need to call someone who isn't my mother.

Q: *Is it true that you are considered to be inhospitable, egotistical, and secretive?*
A: I'm a lone wolf and I am getting to be more secretive. It's not in my nature; it's the fault of this damn fame. I've learned to talk a lot and, almost always, to say nothing about myself.

Q: *That is, like a squid squirting its ink.*
A: That's it.

An Act of Love toward Oneself

GUILLERMO ALTARES/1999

Q : All about My Mother *was the top box office film the week of its release in Spain. Were you expecting this kind of success?*[1]

A : Usually, the indications one gets from the public, particularly on the night of the premiere, are often questionable because this public tends to be of a specialized type; so, even though you can make certain assumptions, in the final analysis it's always a bit ambiguous. However, the two showings, which were the very first two public screenings I had because this time around we only had one press screening, were so warmly received, had such an impact, that it was hard not to believe that the public really liked the film. Because, at that point, they did not have to pretend to like it; and if the audience had been pretending out of a sense of politeness, then they are the best actors in the world. They were under no obligation to like the film since they owed me nothing. If I try to compare what I remember about these first two screenings to the release of *Women on the Verge of a Nervous Breakdown*, which was also a hit but at the level of comedy, this time the success was at a more profound level, the impact was more deeply felt; you could see this in their faces more than in what they were saying . . . Yes, in this case, I did have great expectations for a box office success since the evidence from the test screenings was undeniable.

From *Positif,* vol. 460 (1999). Translated into French from Spanish for *Positif* by Jacqueline Sieger. Translated from French by Paula Willoquet-Maricondi. Reprinted by permission.
[1] *All About My Mother* grossed 142 million pesetas the first week of its release.

Q : *To a great extent, this film is a return to the street atmosphere of your earlier films, given that lately your cinema has been more focused on interiors.* All about My Mother *is a tragedy that all of a sudden turns into a comedy, but it is also very down to earth, imbued at every moment with the streets. This is particularly the case in relation to the characters played by Cecilia Roth and Antonia San Juan.*

A : It's true, there are many exterior scenes, although sometimes that's not the right term . . . What I'm saying is that simply because there are scenes shot outside, it does not mean that there is a street life per se; what it means is that if you leave the houses where the characters live, there is more going on outside, you have to look beyond the windows, and the heroine is far from her milieu. Everything that happens has a street version—or a part of what happens takes place in the streets—and I'm not saying this just in relation to the prostitution of the transvestites, but more in relation to the whole street atmosphere. If, while they are going for a walk, one of them says she isn't feeling good, for me, what I end up staging about them are two insignificant elements compared to the vitality of this entire sequence where twenty-five Dominican or African little girls are jumping rope, mothers are coming to pick up other little girls, four broads in the background are watching the time pass . . . I'm not only showing the street with its problems and particularities, but also the street as a physical space full of life and routines.

Q : *It's really well done in the scene where Penélope Cruz comes upon her father because she wants to go by the little square of her childhood before going to the hospital where she knows she might die. This assimilation of the street, of life, is an important literary and cinematic tradition for us.*

A : And a theatrical one as well. There's an Argentinean song that Chavela (Vargas) sings that says we always return to those places in our past where we loved life. It's totally normal, she's feeling sick. The important thing here is not that she goes by there—even to say goodbye to her family, because after all she will see her mother at the hospital—but that she goes by the square where she played as a child and does not stop. It's a delightful unnamed square, because in Barcelona the squares are all very beautiful, and as far as I'm concerned, I wasn't looking for a specific square but for one that was really popular; I wanted her to just glance at it and to say that that's where she used to play as a little girl. Inevitably, she stumbles upon her father and the dog, but the whole idea of doors onto the exterior, *extra-muros*, is more present here than in my last two films, for example, and more so than in *Flower of My Secret,* which is a film of interiors.

Q : *One of the greatest challenges of this film is its ability to flow between tragedy and comedy, which is not at all easy. The film keeps the audience gripped with all the terrible tragedies and then, all of a sudden, Antonia San Juan speaks and releases the tension to the point of laughter.*

A :   It's really difficult, really daring. When mixing genres, in my opinion, you have to follow your gut feeling; but then there are techniques you can use to avoid favoring one genre over the other. I tend to follow my instincts and sometimes it works out better than others. With time, you master your instincts and you learn to shape them. Above all, the shift in tone should not be forced, artificially planned out to release tension in the spectator, although that is in fact the goal. It has to flow because later it's going to take him into something more important and more terrible. Plus, you have to have a reason. Cecilia Roth's father was telling me that it was like the first twenty minutes of *Saving Private Ryan,* which are really overwhelming because you are put smack in the middle of the tragedy. Here, you are an inch away. Then the film physically opens up onto the city of Barcelona, and this is clearly part of the plot, and onto a new situation, new characters who are not aware of the tragedy, and new energies; and even new genres, although Cecilia remains within the tragic mode since it's her son who has died. Agrado (the character played by Antonia San Juan), is magical, but I never had to make her laugh. That is, the character herself carries both comic and tragic nuances, but they are never forced; she is not made to say funny things just for comic relief, but because it's really that way at the level of the absurd and that is how the character's personal story survives—otherwise she would already be dead. What I mean is, with a kind of optimism that is very funny and often moving, even grotesque . . .

Q : *It's also something we have all experienced in Spanish small towns, when during funerals the tension that arises out of these tragedies can erupt as laughter.*

A :   Which is what gives the impression that the Anglos have invented the genre of *dramedy* so they could better promote *Shakespeare in Love;* we have the drama-comedy, the tragi-comedy, but we've become masters at it, you can see it in our temperament. Every moment of life contains comical elements, because that's life. Once you start observing things, not hypothetically, everyday elements come to light, and very naturally events that occur within a tragic situation start to seem hilarious. That's why I think our culture knows this first hand. It makes me smile that people try to explain why, when it comes to a tragedy like *Romeo and Juliet,* you can't make comedy out of tragedy, and that's why you have to call it a *dramedy,* which makes it sound fancy, like Gwyneth Paltrow herself, but also thin like her. No way; it's a tragi-comedy, that's what you get when the fiercest humor and the most terrible events come together in life; and that's what life is all about.

Q : *Agrado, the character played by Antonia San Juan, is an extraordinary transvestite and also a recurring character in your films. She has never succeeded in completely breaking away from the underground, a place that is not valued very much nowadays but which was very important to her generation. She, who's done theater in the streets and in pubs as much as your character, pays homage to that whole world.*

A : And in Madrid, too, in spite of the fact that Madrid's nightlife is dead. This became clear to me the night of the release of the film; we tried to find a place to hang out after six in the morning; we went to four different places and they were all closed. That's amazing for Madrid, and with Manzano,[2] and it was that way already with the socialists who were trying to turn Madrid into a European city, and you can say they succeeded. It's really sad. But Madrid goes on, and there are places as well as activities that are at the margins of society that continue to pop up, because there was a period in the '80s when this subculture exploded; it was fashionable challenging what was going on and how things were being done. Overnight, stars were born in music, design, photography, and all that seemed kind of unreal, and it fell apart quickly; when someone wanted to write a song or produce something, it was just in order to be the first. The pleasure of doing something for the sake of doing it had been lost, and I think that this underground spirit is starting to come back in the past few years. There are many other places where people are doing different things. Groups tour the little nightclubs, or Antonia gets on a couple of beer cases and does her monologue.

Q : *Cecilia Roth also came out of this wild Madrid nightlife of the early '80s, and she was one of your collaborators in your early films.[3] Why did you invite her back for this film?*

---

[2] José Luis Alvarez Manzano, conservative mayor of Madrid, from the Popular Party.

[3] Cecelia Roth was born in Buenos Aires forty-two years ago and is one of Argentina's most important actresses right now and also very well known in Spain. She was in Adolfo Arista-

A : I thought she had the right measure of a sense of the dramatic blended with the maturity and the sobriety that was needed for the part, while still being a young woman. I really liked what she had done in Aristarain's last film. And she's also a friend. She wanted to get started again, and I thought it was the perfect opportunity. Besides, it was easy to modify the part so she would be Argentinean—which was the only thing we had to account for— and she was the perfect age because I was looking for a young mother, but . . . I had the option of selecting Spanish actresses but they were all a little too young for what I wanted.

Q : *One of the biggest challenges of this film was to connect all the characters and their stories?*
A : When you set a character like Cecilia in motion, since she is looking for someone and is so desperate that she will look for anything . . . What I mean is that her character is a kind of living dead, looking for someone, vaguely, wandering in search of her former husband. She is set in motion through these particular character traits and there is no better motivation than desperation because it can apply to any kind of situation, because in reality nothing interests her. She sees an open door so she goes in; someone says: "Hey, can you drive?" And she says: "Where do you want me to take you?" Because she has nothing better or worse to do, she has nothing to lose, or at least she's not aware of having anything to lose. So it's Cecilia who facilitates all the encounters through her comings and goings. Without her, it would have been much harder to create these interconnections. Cecilia is not only the center of things, but on top of that her search is always in vain, she goes from one house to another . . . So it was easier to use this kind of character to bring together a host of other characters and their particular stories.

Q : *There's this extraordinary sequence where they are all talking together at Cecilia Roth's house.*
A : Yes, that scene made me a little nervous because it breaks with the dramatic power of the woman's confession that horrified Marisa Paredes. She

---

rain's first two films, *A Place in the World,* which won the Concha D'Oro prize at the San Sebastian festival, and *Martin Hache.* With Almodóvar she shot *Pepi, Luci, Bom* . . . (1980), *Labyrinth of Passions* (1982), and *What Have I Done to Deserve This?* (1984). She returned to Buenos Aires and while remaining close friends with the director, she did not work with him until *All about My Mother.*

remembers this child tapping at the window and she is traumatized. The scene begins with the following words: "Listen, forgive me, come back with us." That is, it begins with something really dramatic, but because it involves a group of women, once it's over and they've said what they had to say, over three bottles of champagne and a few peanuts, they let go. In addition to being funny, I see this scene as being typical of a group of women who are relaxed and talking about everything.

Q : *Have you seen Solas?*[4]

A : Yes.

Q : *Granted, it has little in common with your film aside for the fact that it is another recent Spanish film about extraordinary women.*

A : I like it a lot. It's another perspective, a more difficult one, and one that I do not share: the most extreme form of naturalism. How should I put it? There are two films that deal with marginal characters and common people: *Barrio*[5] and *Solas. Barrio* tried to be true to life and have the kind of impact you find in that film *(Solas)* . . . For me, it's like one of those stories, just imagine, where you have five chapters, but the fifth one is missing. It's too short, and there's one missing for the completion of the story, but I can't remember ever seeing a more accurate or impressive portrayal of a father than in this film—the Spanish father, oppressive, repressive, castrating—and he only appears in three scenes and hardly says anything. It's amazing! The powerful economy of this script, and the acting is superb! The daughter is phenomenal and the mother too. And what I also like a lot about it is that, playing off a naturalistic aesthetics, it's not a film in which everybody is talking all the time, it's not forced.

Q : *But these conversations among the women are also present in your film, albeit, at a different level, in a different register . . .*

A : Yes, and when they occur, they are very natural. My film is not naturalis-

---

[4] Sévillan Benito Zambrano's first film, shot with a small budget (about 5 million francs) outside Andalousía and with practically unknown actors (Ana Fernandez and Maria Galiana), but highly praised by critics (and winner of the People's Choice at the last Berlin Festival) and an unexpected hit in Spain.

[5] Another Spanish film that was well received, released in 1998 and directed by Fernando León.

tic, like *Solas,* but once two or three women start talking, their conversation has that natural tonality typical of conversations among women. I find it fascinating to listen to women talk when they are relaxed, or taking a break from work, or when they have decided to do nothing, except smoke cigarettes and take a five minute break, during those moments of tranquility . . . In fact, there aren't many opportunities to listen to them.

Q :   All about Eve *is a film to which you pay tribute several times in* All about My Mother . . . *Even the title of your film is an homage to Mankiewicz.*
A :   I'm paying tribute neither to Capote, nor to Lorca, nor to *All about Eve,* but simply using them as inspiration for my material.

Q :   *Yes, that's true, you tend to incorporate films that you like into your films, like in that famous scene from* Women on the Verge of a Nervous Breakdown *in which Carmen Maura reenacts the dialogue at the end of* Johnny Guitar. *Your cultural references are visible in the body of the film itself.*
A :   I incorporated them in an active way. So they become part of the story, in the same way that this table right here is an objective part of this room. I think that Tennessee Williams deserves to be praised, and as for Truman Capote, well, it's obvious. These are authors that I have greatly admired, like *All about Eve,* as well as Federico García Lorca. But they are tools for the film. Which is to say that Williams's masterpiece, *A Streetcar Named Desire,* is no more a tribute to Williams, who appeals to me tremendously, than Marisa's interpretation of the role is a tribute to Blanche—and she is truly great and right for the part. What matters is that when Cecilia was young she was in the play, and she has already rehearsed the lines she will be repeating, in real life, while pregnant. In this case, however, since in the play she is holding the child in her arms, she is going to turn toward her house and say: "I will never come back to this house, never again," thus abandoning a mate who is her husband, whom she will eventually abandon in the same way. It's as if, all of a sudden, she had rehearsed in this play something that will happen to her in real life. But, on top of that, *A Streetcar Named Desire* becomes a streetcar that runs into the flow of her life, destroying it each time it appears since, after that, she is going to go see it with her son on the same night he dies. Since she says it so spontaneously, it's a play, a situation that has marked her life. It's as if the streetcar had run into her several times, every time it had crossed her life. This doesn't mean that I don't love Williams's

play, but it takes on an active role. The same is true for *All about Eve* and I'm already thinking that it's going to be a woman's film, a film about women who talk, who tell each other their stories, terrible stories. In relation to Manuela's confession, Cecilia's character, who will be a kind of Eva Harrington, is going to have her moment on stage and later again in the dressing room; she is going to tell Margo—who would be Marisa—her story, but it's an awful story, a true story, unlike Eva Harrington's, and above all else, she is a character who has everything except ambition. She is not the kind of ambitious actress who wants to make it on stage: she is a born actress, who knows what to do, but who doesn't have the least bit of interest in acting. She solves her own problems by helping others, and when they misunderstand her she says no, no, and goes on to tell her story. It's the opposite of Eva who is nothing but fiction, unlimited ambition . . .

Q : *Don't you think there are similarities between your cinema and Mankiewicz's, who once said that first he creates the characters, and that then these characters start to live and create their own stories? Like in* All about Eve? *In your films, don't the characters also come before the stories?*

A : Well! *All about Eve* is, above all, an exceptional script, absolutely tight. Everything, absolutely everything in it is planned out to the last detail, like in that famous staircase scene with Marilyn Monroe . . . I've tried several times to reenact this but it's impossible to improve on what he did. From another standpoint, I could do something with the character of George Sanders, who is simply superb; to develop the character from the point at which the revenge search for an Eva begins, and shift the entire focus to this character. It would be the story of a revenge and of its orchestration, the "making" of this revenge. In this case, George Sanders would be very much in love with Margo; because he can't have her, he starts to look for someone to take her place and goes so far as to audition young women who aspire to become artists, until he finds one who is good enough, ambitious, and with no scruples; then, he begins to coach her on what to say and coax her into the dressing room so she can destroy the other woman . . . Just an idea I had. This is just to show you how obsessed I had been with *All about Eve*. Now, it's done and I used the dressing room scene. I like the fact that the writer, the young writer, sees the dressing room scene as the origin of the fiction, the origin which is the story of a bunch of women talking. In itself, this is already amazing, and on top of that, I wanted a child who is preparing to be a writer to witness this scene. This really interests me a lot, a bunch of women talking to each other.

Q : *Were you trying to bring cinema to life within cinema?*
A : It's part of the experience. I don't think it's only that. I don't take it to be something passive. After you see a film, it leaves its mark, like a current that goes between you and the film. This film, then, is now a memory, it has become part of my experience, that is, the experience of having been present and having felt it all. At that point, it's no longer a matter of paying tribute or whatever; you become imbued with your conversations with your father, your mother, your brother, your fiancée, with what goes on in the streets, with what you read, but all that eventually becomes a part of you. Once you have experienced a feeling, that feeling is yours, and that's the one you'll remember. When I create a film, that's how I work, like something . . . well, the truth is, what I create is almost like a theft. Because the same thing happened with *Women on the Verge of a Nervous Breakdown.* While I was putting the film together, I had the sequence from *Johnny Guitar* in mind, and I was stealing that scene from Nicholas Ray because it suited me so perfectly. It was great for me to have Carmen Maura imitate Joan Crawford asking: "Tell me you love me, even if it's a lie," and him reply: "Yes, I love you." It was the ideal thing because, now, she won't hear again this man say I love you. If she does, it is through a recording from far away, and mediated by a film. But the essential thing for me at that point is not to pay homage to Nicholas Ray, but to explain how Carmen, in so far as she is a double, hears her lover tell her "I love you" while the whole thing has already been recorded and is mediated by someone else, and he is not even there. That brutal solitude, that's what I was interested in, and since this scene from Nicholas suited me well, I took it and used it as if it were mine; that's the best way to go about it. To pay tribute to cinema or to make films in order to homage is to make a parasitic cinema; I think you can draw your inspiration from something that was well done or from a scene that captured your interest. You can go about it that way, I think it's okay to use someone else's work. Everybody has his or her influences, from Tarantino to Scorsese, or anybody else. Every being who has a memory has influences. But when people pay tribute out of a sense of adulation, I really don't like that.

Q: *There's another element in that film which you have borrowed from* A Streetcar Named Desire, *and that's when Blanche says: "She always trusts the goodness of strangers," and that's because this goodness is one of the key elements of* All about My Mother.

A: Yes, the goodness of people you don't know. He says "strangers" [in English]. In fact, literally what he says is: "the kindness of strangers," which is to say the goodness, the caring that comes from people you don't know. But then, in my personal rendition, I chose the "goodness of strangers," which suited me because that's one of the themes of the film, the solidarity that the women share. The way these women meet and help one another without realizing it. The truth is, I had hesitated about the title, because there is no feminine version of the word in every language; I had doubts about using the title *La bondad de las desconocidas,* in this case referring to women since they are the heroines of the story. Yes, this expression is absolutely essential and it also indicates the kind of relationship that is being developed among them. This mutual help comes about naturally from these women who are not doing well. What I mean is that Manuela helps them all, but as for her, she finds herself on her knees. She becomes a zombie; this goes to show that in an absurd and violent world, all of a sudden, solutions to problems depend on human relations: with your friends, with those you can call, with those you meet in the streets, in bars; because I think these are the only people who can help you. And here, everyone helps everyone else, in unexpected ways.

Q: *It's true, after the terrible blow she suffers when she loses her son, all she has left are these women she will encounter in the course of the film.*

A: Yes. Because otherwise she would kill herself. They say that in the long and endless list of human suffering, there is nothing as painful as losing a son.

Q: *Did you have a gut feeling about it?*

A: I did, and Cecilia doesn't have a son either. Because she is strong, either this mother is going to kill herself, or she will find any excuse to keep going. All of a sudden she discovers her son's burning desire to know his father, so she takes on that desire and goes looking for the father in order to bring him a few written words and to say to him: "Look, you and I, we had a son, and he is dead." But it looks like a terrible revenge: "Even if you don't believe me, I was thinking about you and these last words I wrote were for you.'' What is fundamentally human is that by helping another, we help ourselves. In reality, when you talk about generosity and all of that, generosity is an act of love toward oneself, because they are actions that bounce back and benefit you; when you do good, it's not that you are consciously doing it for yourself but . . . I don't believe in the kind of generosity that says "I'm going to do something just for you.'' You do it because you feel compelled to do it, and it's good for you. As for her, luckily she finds a reason, an excuse, and she uses it: I'm going to find this man, and I'm going to tell him we had a son, and he is dead, and he was thinking about him. Beyond that, she has no plans. That's the way life is, but while she is looking for him, she moves like a zombie. It's like she has been hit by lightning and is burned up. For example, when Rosa's mother, played by Rosa Maria Sarda, says: "No, we need no one,'' she is rude with her. No one is going to humiliate her; she's beyond pain. She doesn't have enough sensitivity to even feel humiliated. When all in her has been numbed, she can't feel any more pain.

Q : *In addition to that, the memory of her dead son keeps coming back all the time.*
A : He comes up at every turn. She can't talk about him, but not because she doesn't want to, it's just that she can't. And every time she talks about him, she falls apart. It's not hard to foresee. And you have to admit that Cecilia put that across very well. Because, when you have a film that is so overstated, with characters that are so baroque . . . In fact, when you talk about the film, it seems so absurd, half Grand Guignol, half soap opera, and it's really the opposite of that. Plus, I think it's really effective. When we took our time rehearsing, we had the choice of approaching it with sobriety and absolute gravity. In fact, I told Cecilia that I wanted her to avoid crying too often. To be more precise, when she cries, it's already cathartic, like an avalanche that she can't stop, and the rest of the time, it's dry, dry, dry, as if her soul had been stolen. I suggested the same thing to all the others as well, but in a different way. The challenge for all the women, which they understand right away, was to play the roles with a great deal of sobriety. And sometimes they even felt that they were doing too little, or not enough, because the exchanges were so quiet; and I kept saying to them not to worry, not to worry. I think that's what works best, that's what really gives the characters and the story their impact, which overall hangs together.

Q : *That's why when Penélope Cruz is going to have a baby, you have Cecilia Roth say that it's a great day because Videla is in prison and she's going to have a child. Although Cecilia Roth does not have children, she said she felt a real loss, a hurt, because of all her friends who disappeared during the dictatorship years in Argentina.*

A : For many reasons. In addition to that one, it's also because it really did happen during that week we were shooting, children had disappeared. This makes Cecilia's Argentinean side present without also making it too visible. It was a pretext they used with that man. It was like with Pinochet, it came at the right time to make their day and suited Cecilia's Argentinean background, as well as my own personal desire to leave a trace of contemporary history during the shooting. And, it was also about children.

Q : *Some reviewers criticized you for introducing the Lola character at the end of the film, a transvestite played by Toni Cantó, who ends up being the father of both Cecelia Roth's son and Penélope Cruz's; based on what they said, he was not able to meet the expectations.*

A : They are wrong. It's not up to them to judge the range of a character, or how often he must appear, or what needs to be said about him. And whatever you might want to say about him, it's not like he is a Kurtz-like character from *Apocalypse Now*. Lola makes the story up. Lola shows up at the moment that best reflects him, the time of death. For me, Lola is death, and he brings death with him. It's exactly what Cecilia says to him. She meets him because the goal of her search is to meet him. At the cemetery, she tells him what she has to tell him and, strangely enough, while she thought she was going to feel a certain pleasure unloading on this monster, whom she hates, she sees how crushed he is, reduced to dust, crying and full of remorse. And also, Lola represents something that is even more important, and that is the need to reproduce. Who cares who you are and how you are; you have that right. Plus, it's his nature and it's what redeems him. And it's what at the end leads Cecilia to let him know about Penélope Cruz's son. They are a turn-of-the-century family because contemporary families are no longer made up of two people from the same village who have their children in that village. No. Families now take on many shapes; that's also Lola's function, and he fulfills it well. I think it's crucial that the audience be able to see this family, physically see them.

Q: *In this sense, your films have always defended those who are at the margins, different; you have demonstrated that there is no good reason for society to pass judgments like perverse, degenerate, condemnable. For example, here you have a father with breasts . . .*

A: Women get pregnant. To establish a family can mean for two women or two men to adopt a child. Or for a mother to have a child for her daughter. It's very particular to this end of era; everything is radically changing. A family like mine, with four brothers born of the same mother and father, in the same town, is a concept that belongs to another age; the family has survived but has taken on a different shape. The father in *Solas*,[6] yes, he is a horrible father because he stands for the worst of our macho culture. He is a legacy of the Franco period, the worst period in this century. And when he appears it's to kill the women, to beat them up . . . Luckily, now, we can say about a man that he committed an offense. But before, it was as if he had all the right in the world to do that. It's totally acceptable for the character played by Antonia San Juan to make a coat out of a shirt, or to talk about becoming what he dreams of. He can be honest, even pathetic, but he is not hurting anyone.

Q: *Although it is often said that your cinema is better liked in France or in the U.S. than in Spain (your films have always had great success in these two countries), there is no doubt that you have a number of admirers at home as well.*

A: It's true. My cinema is appreciated here too and I notice this when I'm out in the streets. I'm happy with the way my films have been received in Spain. If later they don't award me any prizes or the critics attack me, that's part of the game. But of all things that could happen, that's the least important to me; it's the least significant; it's no big deal. People have memorized the dialogue in my films. Plus, the kind of influence that my films have here is far greater than in other countries, to the extent that we share the language, and this creates a greater complicity with the audience. But it is true that more flattering things are being said about my films abroad.

Q: *Is there a downside to your fame, to the extent that it takes you away from the streets and that it becomes perhaps more difficult for you to observe what's going on freely and anonymously?*

---

[6] In Zambrano's film already mentioned, the father is a horrible, cruel, authoritative, macho figure.

A: There are always difficulties. Because even if I don't think about it, when I go somewhere, people see me and look at me, and it's always a liability because from that point on you are no longer the one doing the looking but being looked at, and I find it a bit artificial to be permeated by the reality brought to me by others. People change when you become famous, even those you know well, and the reality that reaches you is a bit embellished. You have to make an effort to really find out what's going on in life, and you also have to get out there: I go out, I listen carefully, and if I come across professions I am not familiar with, I research it as if I were going to write an article.

Q: *The baroque is an important and essential element in your cinema. Even if some of your characters seem incongruous on paper, once they appear on screen they take on life.*

A: The whole thing hinges on the actors. These characters can exist, even if they seem incongruous, but when you approach them, you do so knowing that they represent extremes. The challenge that I always try to bring to my actors is to make them act as if they were a social portrait. Often, the portrayal is naturalistic but within an overall tone that really isn't. The result is that if you don't overstate things, you end up recognizing the character as if it were your neighbor. That's why it's important to show what is most human about the character, because only that way you'll be able to understand. The same thing happens in this film, where everything has many dimensions; the key thing is to explain how and why the characters are there, and once you do this then people accept it. Particularly if the actors don't overdo it.

Q: *Now that* All about My Mother *is finished and is out, are you finally going to film the novel by Peter Dexter,* The Paper Boy, *which would be your first U.S. film?*

A: It's one of the projects I am working on, but I have to make up my mind in the next few weeks because it's been sitting there while I finish *All about My Mother*. I'm driving myself crazy with this because one day I think I'm going to do it, and the next day I change my mind. I can't decide. I really like the novel, and Peter Dexter himself wrote the script. It's not bad, but it could be improved, and I know exactly how. But I hesitate. I can't get motivated to go to the United States; and even if they give me access to everything there, I know that when it comes to the final cut there are going to be disagreements. Their way of shooting, of producing, too many people making decisions around me. It's the first time that they have proposed a story that appeals to me and that would suit me after this last experience, because it would be a change not only in relation to language, but also in relation to culture and to the genre. Something I have not yet tried: it's like a neo-realist thriller. I have to make up my mind. I'm interested in the story but the script is not yet the way I want it. It could take off. It almost has. I have to decide right away, but also to continue to work on Spanish stories.

All about My Father

SUZIE MACKENZIE/2002

IN THE SUMMER OF, say, 1959, a man, Antonio Almodóvar, left his sleepy little village of Calzada de Calatrava in the province of Ciudad Real, to go and live in the town of Cáceres, a hundred miles northwest, closer and on the road to Madrid. He was just one of millions in Franco's fast industrialising Spain of the 1950s to abandon the traditional country life in the hope of finding work and opportunity in the city—a rural exodus that, ironically, would lead to the subversion of Franco's beloved family values when so many arrived and found that there was nothing for them. With him, Antonio took his wife, Francisca, his two daughters and his younger son Agustín—his eldest son Pedro having gone ahead some time before to board at a school run by the Salesian fathers. We don't know much about this man, Antonio, except that he was undoubtedly a good man, that he could barely read or write, that he worked for most of his life as a muleteer, transporting wine, and that twenty-one years later, in September 1980, the very week that Pedro Almodóvar's first commercial film feature, *Pepi, Luci, Bom, . . .* would open in Madrid, he would be dead from lung cancer.

As he lay dying, his family, wife, daughters, sons, would transport him back to Calzada—to the same street, same house, very same bed, in which he had been born. "We no longer had a home there but my aunt, his sister, still lived in their mother's house and she had the delicacy to invite us, to finish that cycle." Two or three hours before his death, Antonio called for his eldest son. "I remember it very well. My father told me: 'Now you are head of the family. Take care of your mother, take care of yourself, and take care of *el niño,* the baby,' although of course Agustín was now in his twenties but to them he was always the baby." It is a moving scene, you could say a set piece. The dying man bequeathing his legacy to the son he has never understood. The son of whom he used to ask of the mother, "Who does he resemble in our family?" The son who had left home, aged seventeen, for Madrid, with his father's threat ringing, "You are a minor, I will send the Guardia Civil after you." Though of course he didn't. You didn't invoke the police, not if you had lived through Franco's dictatorship. The son who was, is, a homosexual. Did Antonio know? Probably. Did they ever speak of this? Probably not. Antonio was a man circumscribed by his religion. Homosexuality was to him a sin. But he was also a man of his time. Dictatorship enforces silence but it also forces speech, the betrayal of neighbour by neighbour—perhaps its most terrible enforcement. When Pedro Almodóvar says, "As children we would hear stories of people who had been taken out of their homes to the outskirts of their village and shot. This is what makes civil war so horrible. It goes beyond what armies do to each other; it is wars within villages, personal vengeances . . .", it is to this enforcement that he alludes. In these circumstances, if no other, far better silence.

And so he became, Almodóvar says, "like my father." "I never intended it, did not think it would happen, but that obligation fell on me in a natural way and it has become true that whenever there is a problem in the family, everyone comes to me. I am to that effect the patriarch. I couldn't avoid it." That is a tough admission coming from a man whose entire career has been devoted to subverting images of power. He looked after the baby—Agustín is executive producer on all his films since *Women on the Verge of a Nervous Breakdown* (1988). And he looked after his mother, buying her a house in Madrid and later the home she wanted back in Calzada, "on the same street where she had lived as a child." And it was there that he saw something "very curious," something that had not been demonstrated to him before so starkly. "On that street there still lived the little girls that my mother had grown up with but they were all widows now." The men were dead. "Which leads me to think women are much stronger than men."

Strength and, by implication the word not spoken, weakness. That men are weak, that their weakness derives in part from the very power that they assume either voluntarily or that is put on them by their society, is a repeating theme through Almodóvar's films. The men on his mother's street died of an exhaustion of power. "Educated in the fight against poverty," a fight they would not win, they surrendered. There is something noble and pathetic, both, in that image. Men in Almodóvar's films are frequently defeated by a different sort of emasculation. Javier Bardem, that most physical and physically beautiful of actors, ends up in a wheelchair, literally emasculated, in *Live Flesh,* the victim of a bullet from his policeman friend's gun, sure, but equally a victim of his own sexual vanity in seducing his friend's wife. And when, in his impotence, he tries to repeat that exercise of power, he loses more than his balls and his legs. In *Law of Desire,* Eusebio Poncela, playing Pablo, a film director and a homosexual used to exerting control, is defeated first by his own passion and, finally, when he becomes the object of another's passion. He falls in love too late, or too late for this story.

There is a wonderful line in *Law of Desire* spoken by Pablo to his first love Juan: "It is not your fault if you don't love me and it is not my fault if I love you." As spectators we are not asked to sympathise—sympathy is something Almodóvar rarely requires for his characters. He once said, "I have little affection for my characters, for my world, or even for myself." And though maybe now he would retract some of this—in his last four films particularly, I think, he has come to love his characters, and by implication perhaps himself—in a way he is right. Affection is never enough. It may be a start, it is where we all dream of beginning, but it is not a narrative and its end is far from certain. Always, in Almodóvar, there is the warning—don't take a position: it's not your fault and it's not my fault. And a corresponding injunction, follow your dreams. Pursue your fantasy, he says to me, up to the point where it becomes unworkable and then you must let it go. This then is Almodóvar's world, a world of opposing forces: on the one hand restraint, on the other excess, both mediated through his extraordinary sensibility—on the one hand refined, on the other perverse.

He tells me that one of his most potent memories as a child is of his father coming home after a long day's work, sitting solid in his armchair, "like a god," and of the women dancing attendance on him "like slaves." It is an image of unalloyed power and in case I don't get the point, he moves his arms into a position reminiscent of Velazquez's Pope Innocent X. When Almodóvar recounts his father's death he is crying, with restraint, but still weeping. Maybe there is a third element here. For if either I or his interpreter witness his tears, we say nothing—the image of a grown man crying being still something of a taboo.

Almodóvar would understand this as given. In all his work he uses the taboos in culture to undermine them. Which is one reason, I guess, that he opens his latest film, *Talk to Her*—a lyric masterpiece, finer even than his previous great redemptive films, *The Flower of My Secret* and *All about My Mother*—with a scene of a man crying silently. Two men, strangers, sit in a theatre watching a piece by Pina Bausch. Marco, the good-looking one, played by the wonderful Argentinian actor Darío Grandinetti, is crying—observed with some curiosity by Benigno, the fleshy one, played by the equally extraordinary Javier Cámara. Alter egos, we could infer, of Almodóvar himself. So here we have immediately the two classic dramatic genres. Tragedy, identification, as evidenced by Marco's tears. And comedy, distance, as evidenced by Benigno's increasingly curious glances at the weeping man on his left. *Talk to Her,* in spite of its title is a film about silence, and the uses of silence. It is also a film about love. As the plot unfolds, Marco and Benigno, we discover, are in thrall to two women, Lydia and Alicia, who are in comas. As Almodóvar says: "When put like this it sounds almost monstrous." The women cannot speak but their silence elicits in the men a powerful emotional response—in a sense it awakens them. The film also includes a seven-minute sequence of a tragicomic silent movie, *The Shrinking Lover.*

When asked at a recent *Guardian* lecture at the NFT why he had indulged in such a dangerous narrative technique, i.e. to break the narrative thread of the film at midpoint, Almodóvar said this: "I did it to hide something that is going on in the film and something which the spectator should not see . . ." Silence here, then, becomes a way of protecting both his audience and his character. At the same lecture, Almodóvar was also asked about love. "I wanted to show that for utopian love only one person is necessary, that that passion can move the relationship forward." And when I met him, I asked him about this again. Did he really believe it was true? "I am glad that you asked me about that because as I said it I thought that it was just a way of saying something and perhaps not very clearly. Of course I do not think it is ideal if only one person loves, that is a horrible situation, full of frustrations. But what I meant was that for the eventual miracle, love, to happen, it can be enough where just one wants to communicate, he can communicate. So what I am talking about is the strength of that person." I have to say I was not convinced, or not yet.

There is a line in *Talk to Her* which will unfailingly make a modern audience laugh. Benigno, who is in love with Alicia, who is in a coma, says to his new friend Marco, who is probably not in love with Lydia, who is also in a coma: "My relationship with Alicia is better than the relationship of many married couples I know." Of course we think, and Marco, thinks, this is ridiculous. What relationship? Alicia cannot speak. But, finally, I think I understand Almodóvar's point about love—"the eventual miracle." What he is describing is the relationship we have with the dead, who cannot speak to us, but with whom we carry on a relationship until our own death. As he says, it is not over. Not while one person loves.

Which is why I think that *Talk to Her* is a hymn and a homage to Antonio. To the father who didn't speak, or not much, or perhaps only to issue threats to a son whom he did not understand but whom, assuredly, he loved. Almodóvar says this himself. "He loved me more than he did not understand me." To the father who did not live to see his son's success, to see him carry out his dying wishes to provide for the family. Or to see him become, as everyone says of Almodóvar, "the voice of the newly liberated Spain." And to the father who taught him the value of silence. "Fathers are often absent in my movies," Almodóvar has said. "I don't know why." So, to the now absent, yet omnipresent father, who was not, it should be said, a god. In sending Pedro to the seminary in Extremadura, presumably Antonio wanted for his boy the education he never had, and though, Almodóvar says, he was not a political creature—"I don't remember politics ever being talked about in our home"—perhaps he had some sense that the future would be different or anyway that his strange kid was not going to make a life as a muleteer. He must have thought, wrongly as it turned out, the priests would look after him.

Religion was a staple of their life. It was community. It was celebration. Holy Week was all music and flowers and carrying aloft the Virgin. His parents, Almodóvar says, were devoted Catholics, "but in a peculiarly Spanish way. Spanish people take religion as part of their daily life; that doesn't mean that they don't take it seriously, my mother took her saints very seriously. But not mass. The Pope has said the Spanish are a nation of idolators. Well, we are, fortunately and this is good because it's human." The early part of his education he doesn't remember as oppressive. "I don't remember it as being concerned with sin and guilt. In Spain, God as an entity disappeared and what was left was a brotherhood, socialising, parties. Religion helps when you understand it like this, when you don't try to look desperately for some superior who anyway you don't find." At the seminary it was all sin and guilt. "All about original sin, which I have to say is very original. But this is an awful thing to do to boys of nine or ten, to tell them you are guilty just for being born. To engrave in their minds the idea of sin and punishment. Well, luckily I was able to forget that. But psychologically it was very tough." It was also more than this. Eighty percent of the little boys, Almodóvar says, were sexually abused. "About 80 percent of us, yes." He remembers, he says, the dark, the long corridors, and running away—not that there was anywhere to run to. For years he was terrified of darkness. "I remember the priests and how they took my hands and made me kiss them because this is a form of greeting. And I refused and they forced me to." Later at his secondary school with the Franciscans, he says it was better. "But that was because I was older and more able to defend myself." His main refuge was in music, he had a lovely voice, "what they call a white voice," and he sang in the choir. In his films, too, music is often used as a refuge, a way out of a dominant emotion—out of darkness into light.

It is essential to remember that what he is relating here happened to a child. Later, as an adolescent, he could discover his sexuality for himself. And Franco was still alive. In 1970, roughly a decade after the events Almodóvar is describing, Franco passed an act giving police the power to arrest homosexuals "because of the threat posed to society." As Almodóvar says, "It was not a good time to have a sexual orientation that was different." He didn't know he was homosexual at this point: "There were some homosexual experiences in the village when I was about thirteen, fourteen, but these were with bisexuals so I don't think I knew then, I think I accepted it when I was about eighteen. In Madrid I was always able to live in a natural way. I was lucky." That the experience at the seminary destroyed any belief in a God is certain, and it must also have destroyed any faith he had in the exercise of power, in all those "fathers." Maybe at this point, also, he blamed Antonio for his failure to protect him—not from homosexuality, this as he says "is innate"—but from the hands of the abusers. Abuse is, as we are beginning to be aware, rampant. So when Almodóvar speaks here, he is not speaking just for himself.

"Abuse is an old problem which they, the church, don't want to face, but they are having to face it now. It is impossible to contain; it will explode. It is a great problem because the Catholic church does not recognise homosexuality and yet it is probably its greatest promoter. They push celibacy on these young men who want to be priests and naturally the ones who gravitate to the priesthood are the ones who are less attracted to women. Maybe there will be some among them who are asexual. But most of them don't like women because they like men. So what you have is a bit like hunger and being put in a place full of food. Giving the priests the chance to marry is the only way to resolve this problem." He adds: "Also I think that women should be consecrated, as has been done in the Anglican church. This, too, would be a solution to the problem."

It is often assumed that *Law of Desire* (1987) is his most autobiographical film—featuring as it does a gay, cocaine-addicted film director, though Almodóvar never was a coke addict and now takes no drugs at all. But it is in *The Flower of My Secret* (1995), a film about a woman novelist, who is stuck in a rut and a publishing contract, that the narrative tone of his films changes. Up to 1988, and even after the huge international success of *Women on the Verge . . .*, his death as auteur/director of movies had been widely predicted—not least in Spain. His style and most especially his tone—because narrative, as he has said, is tone—was thought to be on the point of exhausting itself. In *All about My Mother,* his biggest success to date, he would even have one of his characters pinpoint this. "I was always excessive and now I am very tired," Lola the transsexual says to his/her former lover just before he dies. Death from exhaustion, or the exhaustion of power, symbolised, of course, in Spain's great national pastime, the bullfight. But Almodóvar, like the bull in *Talk to Her,* has survived.

The change in tone was not a commercial consideration—between 1988 and 1993, seven of the top thirteen Spanish film exports to the U.S. had been directed by Almodóvar. "Growing-up" is how he describes it. "That's something that happens to you in your forties." Now the films, which had always been a mix of realism and stylisation, excessive, melodramatic, given to wild swings of humour, centering on strong female characters and popularising the Spanish subculture of transsexuals, transvestites, as if to blast away the old national stereotypes of dancers and Gypsies, become increasingly linear, less dedicated to aesthetic sensation. What he kept, specifically after 1995, was his subversive use of melodrama, traditionally a conservative genre focusing on the domestic, but in his hands a collision of realism and artifice that makes you laugh and cry.

With each successive film of the past seven years, *Talk to Her* being the fourteenth, he has tightened his emotional control and become more gentle in his vision. Where *Kika* (1993) ends with a sea of bodies and Kika herself driving into the distance with an unknown hitchhiker, *Live Flesh* ends with a birth, one sort of miracle, and *All about My Mother* with the miraculous recovery of a child with HIV.

I asked him at one point about secrets. Every artist needs to have secrets, he told me. "Secrets enrich your life, they can add riches to your work." But secrets also, he says, can become asphyxiating. "For example, if you take sexuality, homosexuality, you don't have an obligation to talk about this but you have an obligation to face it yourself, otherwise you are condemned to a very painful life. That is something people should know." In fact, I wasn't thinking about sexuality. I was thinking about Antonio and about his unusually talented child and how the father must have feared for him. And about the boy growing up in a claustrophobic village: "All I ever dreamed about was getting out of there. I knew that somewhere there was a place for me." All this the father must have known, too, and if it hurt he didn't say. What did Pedro say at another point? "He loved me more than he wanted to control me." Maybe only this is true love. And, of course, the son found his way out, in a way. "Though everything in life is relative, unfortunately," he says.

All children have secrets, he says, they fantasize, and children alone have the ability to make these real. It becomes more difficult later. He surpassed his father and he became the father, though perhaps not the father that in his childhood fantasy he expected to be. But let that go. There are times, he says, when he has longed to be a biological father: "I envy people with children, of course. I would love that. But I am afraid of the life that I could give them. Children need someone to love as well as someone to love them."

The more I think about him, the more I think he is his father's son—Francisca's son too, of course, but not for this moment, not for this film. A bit shy, diffident, a big no-sayer, not at all lazy, and above all honest. I don't think there is one lie in any of his films. You have to say, that is some legacy from father to son. As *Talk to Her* is some tribute from son to father.

The Track of a Teardrop, a Filmmaker's Path

A. O. SCOTT/2002

PEDRO ALMODÓVAR'S NEW MOVIE, *Talk to Her,* which is likely
to cement his somewhat unlikely reputation as one of the leading filmmakers of our time, begins wordlessly, with a performance of "Café Müller,"
a dance piece by the German choreographer Pina Bausch.

Two women, apparently blind, stumble across the stage as their male com-
panions scramble to clear tables and chairs from their paths and to prevent
them from slamming into the walls. In the audience, two men, strangers to
each other, sit side by side, one of them watching, with evident curiosity, the
progress of a tear down the other's cheek.

The story that follows reunites the two men—a male nurse named
Benigno and a journalist named Marco—in a private clinic outside Madrid,
and traces the progress of their serendipitously entwined destinies. Benigno,
who spent most of his life caring for his invalid mother, now devotes himself
to the care of Alicia, a young ballerina left comatose by a car accident. Down
the hall, Marco sits at the bedside of his lover, Lydia, a bullfighter who lies
in a vegetative state after being gored in the ring. The film's title comes from
a bit of advice that Benigno, who regales the silent Alicia with amusing anec-
dotes, beauty tips, and movie plot summaries, gives to the disconsolate
Marco.

"Benigno is not only talkative," Mr. Almodóvar said during an interview
in a midtown hotel on a rainy afternoon last month, a few days before *Talk*

to Her brought the 40th New York Film Festival to a rapturous close. "He tells a lot of stories—related to ballets, to movies. The movie is a kind of glorification of storytelling."

Mr. Almodóvar, in both Spanish and English, is an eager, serious talker, even though his new movie presents decided conversational challenges. "It's a bit of contradiction that a movie that talks about words, communication, human voices is a movie that's difficult to talk about without betraying it," he warned at the beginning of the interview. In at least one very concrete sense, he's right. To attempt even a bald, literally accurate plot summary is to risk not only spoiling some keen surprises but, much worse, falsifying the film's delicate tone and heartfelt mood. Events that might sound outlandish, even grotesque if I tried to tell you about them here are presented with warmth, humor, and sympathy. The film's passionate, brightly colored humanity would inevitably be lost in translation.

Talk to Her, which opens on Friday in New York and Los Angeles, is by far the most complex, layered narrative Mr. Almodóvar has attempted—gliding backward and forward in time, examining the knots and permutations of at least a half dozen thorny, passionate relationships. But somehow, for all the swerves and surprises that follow, that initial sequence of nonverbal, inadvertent communication contains the film's emotional core; it functions as a cinematic overture, gesturing toward themes and states of feeling that will be elaborated, embroidered, and brought together in a work of daunting dramatic scope and breathtaking coherence. Most obviously, Ms. Bausch's blind women prefigure Alicia (played by Leonor Watling) and Lydia (Rosario Flores), shut off from sensory contact with the world. But the emotion that filters from the stage to Marco (Darío Grandinetti), and then to Benigno (Javier Cámara), is also an allegory of both Mr. Almodóvar's message and his method. A work of art speaks to us, and invites us to speak to each other.

"I would have liked to call it 'The Man Who Cried,'" Mr. Almodóvar remarked at his Film Festival news conference. That title, had it not already been taken by Sally Potter for her 2000 film starring John Turturro and Christina Ricci, would certainly have been apt. Marco's tears, which so fascinate Benigno, will also resonate with moviegoers who find themselves caught up in the film's swirl of unrestrained, beautifully modulated sentiment. "One of the ideas that I wanted to convey was a man who cried for emotional reasons linked to a work of art—from seeing a work of enormous beauty," Mr. Almodóvar said, and it is an idea carried forward by the film's tone as much as by its content. His previous movie, *All about My Mother* (1999), which won the New York Film Critics Circle Award and the Oscar for best foreign film, was a powerful and unironic tribute to the great Hollywood "women's pictures" of the 1940s '50s, and to the actresses who brought them to life. *Talk to Her,* which shares its predecessor's interests in grief and in loyalty, is a melodrama in a decidedly masculine key.

Both movies offer audiences something they might not have anticipated from this director: a good, honest cry. In the 1980s, Mr. Almodóvar, who was born in 1951 in the provincial Spanish town of Calzada de Calatrava, seemed to embody the transgressive exuberance of his country's cultural awakening after decades of political repression. Spain's recent history had been lachrymose enough, and there was little time for tears or sighs in the baroque, frenetic world of his films. Of course, there was plenty of sensation—gasps of shock, convulsions of laughter, spasms of liberated desire.

In Mr. Almodóvar's early features, which quickly won him heroic status in Spain and a cult following outside it, the thwarted energies of the Franco era burst out in a riot of color, sex, music, drugs, and decadence. To see *Labyrinth of Passions, Dark Habits,* and *What Have I Done to Deserve This?* was to see the anarchic, libertarian strain in Spanish cinema—long represented by the peripatetic surrealist government-in-exile of Luis Buñuel—restored to its native soil, and to witness both the joys and the dangers of sudden freedom. Those movies were riotous to the point of chaos—pulpy, campy, and gleefully overwrought.

At lunch after the news conference, Mr. Almodóvar happily recalled an early assessment from the American press: "sometimes in bad taste, but never boring." Which was precisely the point: in post-Franco Spain, offending sexual propriety, religious authority, and Fascist family values in the name of pleasure was a therapeutic and a political necessity.

But Mr. Almodóvar has always understood that the pursuit of pleasure is not all about fun. In the early films there were always undercurrents of risk, cruelty, and pain, and an implicit recognition that bodies and feelings, in addition to outmoded social norms, might be damaged by unchained eros. And as the ghost of Franco receded—and the specter of AIDS haunted Europe—he began to explore the darker implications of desire. (In addition to being a central theme in his work, desire is also the name of the production company Mr. Almodóvar founded with his brother and longtime producer Agustín in 1987). *Matador* (1986) and *Law of Desire* (1987) are still headlong, passionate and funny, but they are also disturbing, even a little frightening, in the way they follow the logic of sensual need—the craving for intensity, for novelty, for physical connection—to the edge of the grave.

Those two films, followed by the smashing international success of *Women on the Verge of a Nervous Breakdown,* his great screwball melodrama of 1988, established Mr. Almodóvar as much more than just a naughty provocateur. The habit of provocation for its own sake, however, may have proved hard to break. In the early '90s, it seemed that Mr. Almodóvar risked slipping into mannerism. The sexual insouciance that was so fresh in, for instance, *Labyrinth of Passions* feels forced in *Tie Me Up! Tie Me Down!* (1990) and *Kika* (1994); their light-hearted treatments of stalking, rape, and sadomasochism are less bracing than abrasive.

There is a sense of incipient fatigue in these two films—the bad taste was threatening to become boring after all—which nonetheless have their moments of vibrancy, humor, and insight. They look now like the last bubblings of the post-Fascist cultural ferment—the cinematic equivalent of Chevy Chase's old *Saturday Night Live* news flash: Generalissimo Francisco Franco is still dead.

By the '90s, however, Almodóvarismo, in Spain and beyond, was very much alive. Traces of his influence began to show up everywhere, a notion that elicited a good-natured wince from Mr. Almodóvar. "I do see my influence in some Spanish films," he said, "and even some American films, but I say that with some embarrassment. I truly would not counsel anyone to imitate me, not because I'm so unique, but because I think the way I work is very personal, and also because the kind of material I work with is often on the verge of being ridiculous, even grotesque. Some of my movies became plays, in Spain and in Italy, and they were very successful, but I didn't like them at all. They were very broad and exaggerated. The mistake is that people will think I'll be very happy to go to a play with a lot of drag queens, and I can't tell them that I'm fed up with drag queens, because it might be offensive or it might not be politically correct."

His would-be followers are not the only ones to miss the nuance and sophistication of his work. Like his characters, who keep copies of Djuna Barnes, Tennessee Williams, or Davis Grubb's *Night of the Hunter* on their bedside tables, Mr. Almodóvar is a passionate reader, and from very early in his career he dreamed of adapting novels as various as *The Accidental Tourist, The Silence of the Lambs* and, more recently, *The Human Stain.* The options on those properties, of course, were taken—just think of what the recent history of American cinema would look like if they had not been—though an adaptation of *The Paperboy*, Peter Dexter's melancholy Southern novel, did reach the early stages of production. When Hollywood studios came calling, it was usually with projects like *Sister Act 2* and *To Wong Foo, Thanks for Everything! Julie Newmar*, as if cuddly, commercialized camp, with men in dresses and women in habits, would have represented the logical next step in Mr. Almodóvar's career, instead of a giant step backward.

The Flower of My Secret, released in 1995, marked not only a return to form, but a new direction, as if Mr. Almodóvar, starting from a parodic, camp sensibility, had found his way back to the full, theatrical emotionalism that camp feeds upon and travesties. "I think that emotions have always been present in my films," he says now, "but I'm conscious of a change, of almost deciding that I will concentrate solely on emotions and take away as much of anything extraneous to them as I can, and that takes place as of *The Flower of My Secret*. I now deal with a completely open heart."

"It's not something I had decided," he continued. "It seems imposed on me by my own life and my own experience. I suppose it comes with age; it doesn't really have to do with an intellectual position. I prefer to be unconscious about the reasons. I think it may have to do with a change of a vision, a vision I wouldn't like to say is pessimistic, but which is sad, mournful about life. When I think about my life, I think more about suffering than about joy."

In his last four films—*The Flower of My Secret, Live Flesh, All about My Mother,* and now *Talk to Her*—this sorrow is transformed into tenderness and beauty. There is something deeply consoling in Mr. Almodóvar's mature vision, and the consolation comes from a deep faith in the power of art. To an extent more unusual in the movies than in life, perhaps, his characters define themselves, and reach each other, through their experience of books, movies, theater, and music. In *High Heels*, Victoria Abril's character expresses her rage toward her mother by citing a scene from Bergman's *Autumn Sonata*. The lovelorn romance novelist in *The Flower of My Secret* dissects her romantic predicament with reference to *The Apartment*. The desperate lovers in *Matador* find their violent passions mirrored and inspired by Gregory Peck and Jennifer Jones in *Duel in the Sun*.

The examples proliferate, and they are not confined to movies, or to actually existing works. (At the center of *Talk to Her* are excerpts from *The Shrink-*

ing Lover, a wonderfully bizarre black and white silent film directed by Mr. Almodóvar himself.) Nor are they displays of erudition for its own sake, or attempts to cannibalize cultural prestige.

Sometimes they operate at an almost subliminal level. At one dramatically crucial point in the new film, Mr. Almodóvar noted, the camera glances at a copy of *The Hours* by Michael Cunningham underneath a telephone. "On the cover," he said, "you see a detail of a painting of a body under water, with her hand resting on the water." "This apparently casual image has a deep and complex resonance. "On one hand, this is a confession that I love *The Hours,* and that I would have liked to have made the movie, but they already did it. But it is also about the theme of death and water. Rain becomes for Benigno a point of entry into the world of Alicia's coma. Obviously I don't talk about all these meanings because it's not necessary to understand them, but when I'm making a movie it's necessary to surround myself with a lot of images that have a lot of meaning for me, and to the story."

And the story, as a result, is saturated with meaning and thick with feeling beyond what the viewer is able to analyze or the filmmaker to explain. *Talk to Her,* like the Pina Bausch pieces that serve as its bookends, and the gorgeous Caetano Veloso song that is its centerpiece, seems to possess a soul of its own, compounded of gravity and elegance, not explicable or reducible to anything else. "This movie represents something very intimate of myself," Mr. Almodóvar said at the end of our interview, "something that even I feel embarrassed to talk about, some part of myself that I don't even know how to verbalize."

Yet it communicates perfectly. As I stood up to leave, Mr. Almodóvar offered to autograph my copy of the soundtrack CD, which includes Mr. Veloso's song, as well as Alberto Iglesias's lush, melancholy orchestral score. As the elevator doors closed, I glanced down at the cover, and noticed the message Mr. Almodóvar had written above his signature, a private communication I am happy to pass along. "Cry," it said.

INDEX

CONVERSATIONS WITH FILMMAKERS SERIES

PETER BRUNETTE, GENERAL EDITOR

The collected interviews with notable modern directors, including

Robert Aldrich • Robert Altman • Theo Angelopolous • Bernardo Bertolucci • Jane Campion • George Cukor • Brian De Palma • Clint Eastwood • John Ford • Jean-Luc Godard • Peter Greenaway • John Huston • Jim Jarmusch • Elia Kazan • Stanley Kubrick • Fritz Lang • Spike Lee • Mike Leigh • George Lucas • Michael Powell • Martin Ritt • Carlos Saura • John Sayles • Martin Scorsese • Steven Soderbergh • Steven Spielberg • Oliver Stone • Quentin Tarantino • Lars von Trier • Orson Welles • Billy Wilder • Zhang Yimou